Coyote's Song:
PART TWO

Coyote's Song:
PART TWO

MATTHEW THEISEN

COYOTE'S SONG: PART TWO

iUniverse books may be ordered through booksellers or by contacting:

iUniverse
1663 Liberty Drive
Bloomington, IN 47403
www.iuniverse.com
844-349-9409

ISBN: 978-1-6632-4882-4 (sc)
ISBN: 978-1-6632-4883-1 (e)

Print information available on the last page.

iUniverse rev. date: 12/07/2022

Contents

Summary

Coyote was given the duty of finding a non-corporate story for Lady Nature. He met with Puck, who was psychically delivered to a mental prison by Sheik Dabu of Iabud. Coyote, during a cycle of prayer and fasting in a thicket of woods, believes he is the next Vishnu. A new, young Coyote rises and in a desert raids the drug-parcel of partying campers.

11

Mephisto's War

Puck was turning to shades of ivy green
from watching acts on a wall-monster screen.
Some of it centered on his sordid past,
due to fine dropsy and a hunger-fast.
Visions roiled in each other without seams
as punishment for pranking people's dreams,
or instilling a wakened psychosis
with illicit laughing Soma doses.
Now that it clobbered Puck to a moon-calf,
he found it difficult to have a laugh.
Lady Levity took the Sheik's tribute
to keep Puck's spirit caged, deranged, and mute.
At least they gave him his own phantom-cell,
and perhaps his visions would start to quell.
He saw the time when he dosed a rooster,
who soon believed his cry was the booster
for the sun's disc to arise every dawn,
controlling light and the food of the lawn.
Puck found no joy in viewing his past work
flowing about him, his mind gone berserk,
so he began to pray to his mistress,
but only conjured words in his address
that was a nonsensical gibbering,
which he was unaware had the bearing

to summon Mephisto down a dark hall
and grandly appear on the dungeon wall.
He had quit hunting old Yote when the sight
of him becoming Vishnu reached its height.
Gravesend's fiends, sent with Mephisto, dallied
at a political show that rallied
extreme groups to a single perspective,
so the fiends played at being detective,
gathering information for their boss
to melt the useful alloy from the dross.
Mephisto's desire as a free agent
changed to wanting to control a regent.
Beams of light showed through Mephisto's lank frame,
and he held some contracts for wealth and fame.
He adapted to being body-free,
and was ambitious for a high-degree.
Mephisto: "I see you have been released
from your job, and Sheik Dabu has you leashed.
Selling you out gave her no compunction
because self-control is your malfunction,
it always has been and always will be.
But I admire that trait, so sign with me
and I will turn you loose to spread glory
of the new era's unwritten story
I steer, though do not micro-manage laws
of atoms or Adams like Yaweh's Cause.
Over-organization hurts each sense,
posing stupidity as innocence.
I considered scheming tricks to hurt you,
but chose to offer a role in my crew.
We will reshape the laws and give them words
without regulations, hired by shepherds
who do not want our work traced back to them,
so we can smoothly glide through each system.
Leaders and elite of every nation
are scared of our gathered information,

so none of them will dare to interfere,
as they instill in their herds a great fear
of the wrath of their lords' doing a cull
for messing with business as usual.
You can fool with the minds which I dictate
should be full of love or consuming hate.
You will have your freedom, but be aware
that if you think this is Hell, a worse lair
is waiting for you upon betrayal
of me or those who put themselves on sale
to us, though I expect no loyalty
beyond the wealth that buys your fealty.
Capitalism taken to extremes
sells people like products in fulfilled dreams.
Sign with me and be free of these nightmares,
going back to your fun of pranking snares."
Because Puck was skewed by fated brain-stirs,
anything was better than wall-monsters,
who seared synapses of comprehension
between ideals and the third-dimension,
where the shadows fell that contained no fun,
but continued showing doom being spun.
Mephisto gazed at the wall, shook his head,
and with mock ripe words of concern he said:
"Literature students read too much gloom
about the many ways we find our doom.
They become morbid and weave nations' tales
of how even the greatest effort fails.
At least the Roman Catholics offer
hope, forgiveness, and Heavenly coffer,
but they have been replaced by consumption
of poisons that can have no redemption,
so the tales also become polluted,
as it reflects the world which they looted.
Why should you not also get a good share?
By signing with me, you pay your own fare,

and can build something that does not rely
on writers' webs that glue you like a fly
to roles you dislike, ending in this joint
where a method to madness has no point.
Come here, Bunny, and show him happiness
if he chooses to leave awful duress."
A blonde, German milk-maid lass stepped forward
from the tunnel into Puck's prison-ward.
She smiled at him and waved a kind greeting,
then she left and he groaned at the fleeting
image dissolving to colored atoms,
luring Puck to be one of the Adams
who start a new species with the wisdom
and experience that makes angels hum.
Puck and she could guard their own paradise
from those evicted by ambition's vice,
who raid others' homes with cupidity
because their god preferred stupidity
and obedience in the chosen few,
whom use bribes and extortion in their crew
to construct new Edens on others' work,
with self-fulfilled prophecies where shades lurk.
Jesuits forced natives to learn Latin,
now teach to knob-push through worlds that flatten
life into gibberish computer codes,
learning how to act in each system's modes,
which the uninitiated fail at,
so arcane screen-worlds are ruled by a brat.
The elite and their protégés confuse
vernacular ability to choose
the path of achieving a higher-state
beyond influence of karma and fate;
the elite choose to steer artificial
money and a synthetic ritual.
Tales were moribund, dissected, retold
in a market where anything was sold.

Invented memories were passed along
as terrors, scripture, or a nation's song.
Switching roles for screen-rewards seemed pointless,
as did serving those pretending to bless.
Thus far, Puck had been a tiny icon,
like some goofball from *The Satyricon*.
This Armageddon stuff was serious,
so why not release the imperious
urge to stage the apocalyptic shows
everyone fit to a personal pose?
Puck signed the flimsy sheet held out to him,
laughing dementedly, gleeful and grim.
Mephisto waved his arm, and the walls fell,
and Puck's senses recovered from the spell
that had placed him in a gray twilight haze,
which unleashed him for the next cycle's phase.
He saw various villains collecting
good people to manage, while selecting
products for them to consume harmony
and build credit in the economy.
Artificial intelligence arose
to herd people to their preprogrammed rows
as links in the villains' karmic-whiplash,
smiting those with bad credit and no cash.
Some of the storylines had bravery,
which fought against imminent slavery,
while good people pled for a stable life,
their minds merging with Edens free of strife.
Women were the first to desire their own
creations from the seeds rebels had sown.
As war-lines drew close, they began to swerve
when the females refused to meekly serve:
they had their own tales to chant, sing, and dance,
both of royalty and illicit chance.
Storyline collisions brought forth the souls
of contraries manipulating roles.

Supporting forms were given to each star:
perfect proxy-lives promised from afar.
Puck saw all this in a few moments' flash,
then the view of multitudes turned to trash.
Puck: "That is my job now, to make it boil,
stirring up good people's minds so they spoil
their Eden by excluding another
from good grace, like Lilith as a mother.
It will not be like the pastoral odes;
the modern farmers dump pig-manure loads
to add pollution to minds in screen-acts,
which reinvent truths by warping the facts."
Puck was irate that his techniques of art
evolved to synthetic tools lacking heart.
Mephisto understood Puck's annoyed theme,
so the fiend said, speaking of the world's dream:
"Classroom performances teach words to sing
that children can grow to do anything
they set their minds to, except drink water,
because corporations bought that charter,
and pollute it with the by-product waste
of what is taught to consume as good taste.
They learn to like artificial flavors,
and how to game the systems for favors.
Taught to play as if their souls are the stakes,
your nature's dropsy becomes hybrid fakes,
geared to open minds to the messages
from deceptive, subliminal sages.
The new Soma of Eden either quells
people into domesticated spells,
or stirs rebellions rampaging down streets,
depending on how 'tis rigged by elites."
Mephisto smiled and his eyes glowed a sheen
as he conjured an erupted town scene,
and said: "The Yanks' message-makers were hired
to prevent this nation from being fired

by those who have been cheated by their Sheik,
and his rumblings of war begin to peak.
Yanks have boots on the ground to steer the crowd
and assassinate chiefs who are too loud,
but counter-social media programs
are used for subversion and staged pogroms.
The protestors' minds are like mirror-panes,
reflecting what is put into their brains:
telling them to feed the Sheik his vices,
which is worthy of their sacrifices
in hopes one day they too can be raunchy,
being served by those who face life staunchly.
Consuming warped facts can lead to bladders
full of gall and intrigues that change matters.
Some are subtle with their eructations,
others belch fat and lazy temptations.
By using your skills, you can get vengeance
through rearranging Iabud's essence:
caught in the throes of a false self-image,
tearing themselves apart to vow a pledge
of obedience to stability
I concoct with fiendish ability,
so that they feel resurrected and whole,
and a superior race of people.
'Tis all the philosophy they need know,
the rest are mere pageantries of my show:
ceremonies, incantations, and runes
specially designed to channel my boons."
Puck kept pace with the quick strolling devil,
their height slightly above the street-level,
near the drones taking pictures of state foes
for facial profiling to smite them woes.
The crowds carried banners and hurled missiles
at troops who split ears with sonic whistles.
A wave of tear-gas induced savage howls,
and Mephisto looked like a beast who prowls.

The fierce crowd surged against the soldiers' shields,
but neither side broke on the battlefields
of the wealthy district being looted,
and Puck thought it was a job he suited.
If humans chose this irrational hate,
he would be happy to alter their state
to a degenerate misguided lust
for a tyranny based on the unjust.
As if Mephisto understood Puck's head,
the fiend produced a small gadget and said:
"With these buttons I control all their wits,
and can induce epileptic-like fits
in the leaders who steer both of the sides
through screen-commands, urging the human tides.
Beams were installed to provoke a seizure
like Saul of Tarsus had, lacking pleasure,
when Jesus zapped Saul with a bolt of light
as he went to whump Christians with a blight.
I will keep this as a last solution
if we fail with other mind-pollution.
The Yanks were hired to direct the mob's rage
against a neighboring nation's image,
which the Yanks carefully cultivated,
and will soon have the hate elevated
towards those deemed linked with a demon-faith;
you shall hijack the show as a tech-wraith.
Yankees, with funds from Iabud's elite,
bought most of the rebel guides, who will bleat
that Iabud's woes are caused by a state
who rile the protestors, dispersing hate,
while cheating Iabud's economy,
which stirs unpatriotic infamy."
Puck: "I suppose hate towards that nation
has something to do with Yanks' oil-ration,
leaving the street-fighting poor with a bag
full of the Sheik's vehemence, like the plague

of contrary winds from Lord Aiolos
given to homeward-bound Odysseus.
The poor must enlist for the monarchy
or tried for sedition and anarchy.
I imagine the physical cages
here are much worse that the psychic rages
I suffered when I roamed from laughter's track,
when she abandoned me to somber wrack.
The laws of karma work in nature's curves:
my ex-Lady will get what she deserves.
I refuse to be one of those poor fools
directed by the masters of fish schools."
At this, Mephisto could not help but smile,
though he turned his head, at Puck's lack of guile.
Was he really such a simpleton
to be reshaped like ore that is molten?
He was dumber than the fools on the street,
all because he thought revenge would be sweet.
He was more crazed than if on eye-dropsy,
like sailing on a revenge tidal sea
where he did not care if he was left blind
by eye for eye, which Mephisto designed.
'Tis said the very soul is in the eyes,
and his device would tell them countless lies.
The crowd rallied to push the armed forces
to a side-street, like corralling horses.
While the mob's first line held the troops at bay,
the second was like a wave on a cay
that is low-lying and swept by typhoons,
which build tide on tide like desert sand-dunes.
Mephisto watched and thought: Ah, this is good;
they do not burn down their own neighborhood
like I have seen other idiots do,
as if it made the wealthy pay their due.
Stores were raided as were financial firms,
as crowd segments broke like dissected worms,

and went their business ways of pillaging,
'til their leaders could gather the raging
sections and reform them to stay focused,
like a machine oiled and scrubbed free of rust.
Mephisto waved his hand, building a scene
where a woman typed codes to aim the spleen
and vitriol of the crowd to a fate
which had its gall pointed towards a state
the Yankees considered bad for business
through an Ayatollah's version of bliss
that his people consumed, making the Yanks'
market shrink, which earned the naughty some spanks.
The fiend: "She is set to tell the leaders
of the crowd, via computer-feeders,
to have the protestors shift through some gears
to support Sheik Dabu and all his peers,
except his cousin-in-law, a scapegoat,
the crafted symbol of royal bloat
which seams through the nation's hierarchy:
an immolation to stop anarchy.
When she gets her last orders from her chief,
you can do your duty as a mind-thief
so they sacrifice the third-dimension
for a false screen's promised resurrection.
They bought some agents of great potential
in Nari, the Sheik's foe, both official
bureaucrats and covert army agents
ready to replace Nari's top regents
with the chief military general,
who pimps his country like a common trull:
for protection by the powerful states,
he will crush rising democracy traits.
During deepest night we shall implement
the propaganda to have their minds bent.
The show is almost over for the day,
they go home and check what their leaders say

to do on the morrow, which the Yanks' scheme
directs for Sheik Dabu's oligarch team.
For now, let us enjoy the violence
before it turns to chaotic nonsense.
You see that man with his head well-covered,
whose rock brought down a drone while it hovered?
He once planned to be a Muslim cleric,
but his knowledge and pride began to prick
his teachers who tried to control learning,
and could not rearrange his discerning
metaphors bonded to their history,
so he, unaware, joined with my story.
Maybe if he knew the truth of the tale
he would continue to protest and rail,
for the clerics treated him shabbily,
so might greet their usurpation with glee.
He is a street-fighter and joined a het,
but he may be useful as my prophet.
He is caught between learning the new dance
between old oppression and decadence,
which is hung as a label on the West,
but staying crushed down is not always blest.
He just whacked a soldier over the head,
which makes another martyr who is dead
at the hands of a new faith which rises
to claim the storylines with their prizes.
Ah, now the soldiers have my man circled.
Will he survive their attack or be culled?
Here come his goons to rescue their leader,
easy to guide by computer-feeder,
being simple-minded and quick to fight.
Oh, there she is who makes my dark life bright!
She slips her hand beneath the troops' face-shields
to blast the pepper-spray bottle she wields,
and the soldiers reel back, sicker than Hell.
She will be a linch-pin under our spell.

She believes in social conscience and thinks
to form a policy that never sinks.
A true believer whom I much admire
for diving in the muck of this street-mire.
Taniah is her name, and her parade
of light is dimmed by my man's ego-shade.
Saiid, the hero who was just rescued,
coerced her group to join his, then he skewed
all their non-violence into mish-mosh,
so they fight against the hounds of the posh.
She refused to take him as a lover,
and foolishly she has no face-cover,
thinking she can be up-front in debate,
instead has become a foe of the state.
Her goal was peaceful diplomatic deals;
'tis fun to wreck those of high ideals.
She has just become an accessory
to a murderer who is not sorry.
Look at how her face falls yet is livid
with rage at troops, while her doom is vivid
scenes in her mind, knowing she is fitted
to a role as a beast who is pitted
against the army-dogs they now turn loose,
and the show just got some energy-juice.
Using water-cannons in desert land
lacks even more foresight than these fools planned.
The buggers will just scoop up the liquid
to sell on the market to the high-bid.
'Tis amazing how wretched they become,
and the elite are surprised a war-drum
is pounding among those whom the elite
told so many lies to with hearts that cheat.
The dogs which are unleashed on the riot
are only half-trained, and their mean diet
may well include their handlers or shock-troops,
for Heaven's hounds discriminate no groups.

The police desire to do it their way,
but the army wants to direct the play,
as does each sundry covert agency
on Earth invested in the regency.
The protestors have just taken rifles
from troops they cornered and crushed to stifles.
They may not know how to use the weapons,
or have live ammo against the Sheik's pawns.
They fire so randomly they kill their own.
This is like a religion's riddle koan,
which has no answer, yet spurs laughing thought
of how to build enlightenment we sought,
but instead tear the whole thing to pieces
so we can rearrange image leases.
A promise of oil-stocks bought machetes
for frontlines of protestors that steadies
itself for attacks from the devil dogs,
as waves of tear-gas float like tidal fogs.
The screams and retching are a symphony
among howls and chants that are not phony.
Yet 'tis a laugh these conducted riots
are orchestrated by non-patriots,
for though both sides believe in their prophets,
their songs are led by those seeking profits.
There is Akeem, the stud whose face appears
on web-sites to recruit subversive peers,
especially among global females
who want life to be *Arabian Tales*.
Notice he is further back in the throngs,
though not a coward, 'tis where he belongs,
because ring-leaders wish him no scarred harms
'til he is older and lost his sex charms.
Ah, there he goes, taking off his white shirt
to make him seem he can come to no hurt:
an invulnerable icon of lust
calling for revolution that is just.

His web-site ratings just marked a new high,
and made his foes frightened to have him die
with his blood on their hands, which would upset
his heart-throbs around the world who regret
one handsome man's death over thousands dead.
I love it when emotion is mlsled.
Taniah was offered her own web-site,
as a peaceful counterpoint, but her spite
for staging beauty contests was her flaw,
thinking she could win through use of the law.
Well, we saw how good that turned out for her,
she is now attacked by a snarling cur,
and is nearly trapped by troops with night-sticks,
who abhor women involved in this mix.
Taniah's bodyguards protect her flanks,
she is their idol and they give her thanks.
When one is made rich and praised for bad art,
one may think their paying crowd none too smart,
and treat them like dog scat when one performs,
while the content misleads as does its forms;
or believe one is worthy of that height,
and any who doubt is guilty of spite.
Taniah lost her mild humility
by being the face that wrecks the city.
Her guards beat the troops to a bloody mash,
and a camera lens gets a nice splash,
which will appease the Yankee audience,
like Olympian gods, through Yank science;
which is akin the elder gods' machine
that viewed and manipulated each scene.
Americans love their celebrities,
and Taniah knows how to dress and tease
men to think she is more than a mere flirt,
though is interesting under her skirt.
Plus, she is a relief from the male throngs,
and her voice is pleasant in scripture songs.

A fierce dog just flung himself at her throat,
but a guard stepped in with a quick garrote,
and strangled the mutt to its afterlife.
Is Taniah's face damaged by the strife?
Her guards hover round so I cannot see
if her ratings just dropped during the spree.
Akeem is fighting his way to her clique
where cameras stay, for she is their pick
as the evening star while night approaches,
and Akeem is jealous that she broaches
on his quality time, and takes his cue
so he can say he led to her rescue.
Night is time to stop for the ring-leaders
told to do so by computer-feeders,
which the Sheik allows the rebels to use
to work a head of steam, then by a ruse
aim it Nari, a once-friendly state,
by subverting every rebels' screen-slate.
And that is where you come in, little pal,
when the Sheik goes to the Yankees to sell
Iabud to war with Yank munitions,
and oil-blood is the sum of fruitions.
Let us go to where the chief-hacker hides
in Switzerland, where she avoids the tides
of humanity teeming round this mess,
which I will soon control to curse or bless."
Mephisto and Puck found a straight network
that beamed to where a woman sat at work,
watching on-screen Iabud's civil war,
prepared to type-in the computer spore
which would change the direction of the fight,
like a script for a film someone could write.
Mephisto solidified to content,
and told Puck to prepare for the event
of possessing the covert courier
delivering to the screen-warrior

the codes to redirect the social feud,
and march to war with a glad attitude.
Mephisto: "Though my form is firm, they lack
means to see my fourth-dimension attack.
Her vision is strained from staring at screens,
and I have already planted the means
to have her insert my own index code,
more modern than newt's tongue or eye of toad.
You switch the eye-drops the courier brings
to salve her pupils that the screen-glare stings,
with your dropsy that makes peons of kings.
I salvaged the potion from your flesh wreck,
and it has stayed potent, not turned to dreck.
She will not be aware, due to your dram,
the new codes she instills is my program.
She shall believe she soothes her scorching eyes,
while we switch their fictions to our own lies.
I overrode the master monitors
with a worm virus that spreads like germ-spores.
The Yanks will have to cut losses and run
before 'tis traced to them and are undone.
Then my program shall be free to play out,
and Heaven and Hell will gush forth a spout.
There he is, with the orders and eye-drops.
Get into his form and open all stops."
Puck slid into the courier with ease,
and feeling in the body helped appease
the discomfort of serving at the whims
of a fiend who branched through computer limbs.
The body Puck took over was well-built,
and he was tempted to stay sheathed full-hilt,
but knew his reputation was at stake,
even if it 'twas an oath to a fiend-snake,
so Puck switched her medical eye-drops with
dropsy that draped the genesis of myth.
Puck handed the code-pack to the agent,

then left the body to watch the advent
of a new millennium taking shapes,
which served the Sheik sour wine from wrathful grapes.
Puck thought with a cool and clear brevity:
Next on my list is Lady Levity.
Service to Mephisto can give me that;
I must honor him and not be a brat.
But what shall I do about my body?
I have no content, simple or gaudy,
so long as my shell remains upon Earth,
which makes my spirit feel an intense dearth.
I can work no mischief at her until
the shell I had dissipates by her will,
then the fiend can have his potter's wheel spun
and shape me a cruel, imposing one;
but if Lady Levity knows I plot
against her, my body and soul shall rot.
She may already be filled with intent
to smite me with terrible punishment
for signing Mephisto's service contract,
because she easily has my moves tracked.
Why do all masters lie about a bliss
in return for dedicated service?
Puck looked at Mephisto with that last thought,
as the devil disappeared, leaving naught
but a visible darkness which spun round
as if shrouds of black energy were gowned.
Puck felt like part of his reasoning soul
left with the fiend to pay Puck's freedom-toll.
Thus, the horrors did not affect his mind,
and compared to what wall-monsters designed,
Puck was happy he was not in that cell,
and got revenge with a computer-spell.
He was free, so it was time to locate
his body with hopes that he could dictate
the shell's movements with brain activity,

then he would deal with Lady Levity.
He paced back and forth in the covert room:
he missed something and the lack could bring doom
upon his head, or at least increase woes,
but did not think he made too many foes
in a world fighting over illusions
using betrayal, blessings, and collusions.
Puck's mind-library was purged of bookshelves,
like modern people who sang of themselves,
prophesied by the self-obsessed Whitman,
whose poems were truly American
nauseating lessons how to consume
and reproduce oneself as a volume.
Though there were enough bad poet/sages,
most switched to narcissistic images
where they could play like Yaweh at controls,
and extort others to pay for good roles.
This world of wild, schizophrenic vision
paved the means for one almighty version.
Puck was vaguely aware it had that end,
but had other matters he must attend.
Though his subtle reasoning was impaired,
he trusted his instincts, yet was still scared
of Gravesend and his fiends hunting stray sprites
either to conscript them or instill frights
which would keep them from war-lines being drawn,
too terrorized to fight the demon-spawn.
Puck left the site, searching for tunnel doors,
and by avoiding the main corridors,
where the spirits flew in thick, beamed passes,
gathered as psychic energy masses,
Puck was able to skim across waters
and land without tolls or haggling barters.
He paused for a moment to watch the dreams
of gathered consciousness arrange for streams
which poured humanity throughout their lives,

setting scene acts and dialogue that thrives
on current trends and latest catch-phrases.
Puck would have liked to mess with those phases,
but he needed his body on the mend
before 'twas stolen by one like Gravesend.
Puck was small-time when it came to intrigue,
but serving Mephisto rose Puck a league,
though he was unaware of how wary
his focus should stay, he must not tarry.
He looked at the gathered souls like ripe fruit;
he could give it to his Lady as loot,
and thus make amends for their falling-out,
but the thought of revenge-taste made him stout.
Why should he apologize for some wrong
she invented in her head as a song,
which blared and replayed some sort of misdeed
that plucked him from her garden like a weed?
So far as Puck knew, no sin had been done:
'twas a standard task, committed for fun,
and when it went bad, she was of no help,
so Puck gave the gathered souls a curse-yelp,
and went on his way, feeling no remorse,
with thoughts of vengeance keeping him on course.
His soul was drawn to his body to fill
the void which could not be cured by a pill.
He saw his atoms had a drudge-like spin
at the hospital where Puck was bound in,
staring at a television program,
beside a patient who spoke of its sham:
"What can one say of the anti-heros
of this culture, who are mini-Neros?
They fancy they are great poets onstage,
paid to blast dead white poets with hate-rage.
Then 'tis taught, because 'tis the posers' truth,
that storylines must be purged without ruth.
One may ask if it is worth fighting for.

The ancient gods used as a metaphor,
or in lyric passages on nature
have no depth in a world lacking pasture.
Yet when one thinks of the ills done by farms,
sharecropping, slavery, and other harms,
'tis difficult to make the untrue stick
that we would be happier if rustic.
The romantic charms of country idylls
are replaced by contests to be idols.
Rome's Catholic Church has slowly dissolved,
like the pantheons from which it evolved.
The study of a serial-killer
has replaced the poets as a pillar
of society's vision, and fills needs
to rebel against the corporate seeds,
who sow to make monsters for their own use,
fitting their audience for vile abuse.
Just like the ancient gods unleashed their wrath,
conglomerates use subliminal math
to put forms in the heads of predators,
and keep people flocking to web-like stores
to partake in their brands of energy
to be parts of a subsidiary.
The anti-hero centers on the stealth
of the subterfuge means to gaining wealth.
Just as Apollo and Aphrodite
chose sides at Troy's war, with Zeus the mighty
as final judge of the awful conflict,
so corporations have their chosen picked.
Like gods used delusions in the combat,
whether in battle or during a chat,
which made humans retreat or charge head-long,
subliminal messages guide our song,
crafted by our own peers as oblations
to buy good lives from the corporations,
which are kind of a shepherd to the herd,

censoring the old songs to not be heard.
If humans ever re-connect those links,
the new *deus ex machina* would have kinks
thrown in it by a true anti-hero,
whose monkey-wrench would render them zero.
It is funny how Platonic numbers
awaken the wrath of one who slumbers,
and dreams without shapes from digital forms,
and then awakes to be the force of storms.
What have we truly built to take the place
of our fictional past, which we erase
for fads of the latest machine lyrics,
or told we are evil and need the pricks
of conscience to buy into a lifestyle,
lest judged by an Inquisitor trial
for having priorities than slaughter
of old traditions, such as clean water?
I like you because your ears can listen
even as the screen shapes things that glisten
through our brain-patterns, causing the spasms
in appetitive souls by phantasms.
That is what Thomas Aquinas would write,
though outdated by philosophy's blight.
You pay attention, though catatonic,
like when I had strong gin and weak tonic
with Shakespeare's ghost, and I bought all our drinks,
which landed me here, riddling with a sphinx,
also known as a screen with secret codes:
television and Oedipal crossroads,
where I fight personality auctions
and parent conglomerate adoptions.
The most digits used to transmit a face
wins Plato's metaphysical math-race,
and perhaps achieves a Heaven of sorts
in scoreboard records of Saint Peter's courts.
The most points win an empty form:

yellow, white, black, or red brag-up a storm
of vacuous sound, impotent fury
for faithful hues to score in a flurry
of shallow rerun shows in their color
to make the audience's wits duller,
who also have agendas channeled-in
for work done by an influential spin
with a catch-phrase or a shirt one contrives
celebrities to wear in proxy-lives.
You drool a bit, here are some clean tissues.
I like how you pay heed to the issues
which I bring up, for most think I am crazed,
in and out of dimensions that are phased
to link and coincide with the versions
the elite choose to sell in dispersions
as the momentary truths of fusion
with what is the marketed illusion."
Puck slipped into his body as a voice
told his human ears of the latest choice:
a man had been found beyond all prophets,
whom Iabud loved for promised profits.
Puck looked at the screen and saw his master
had found the means to control disaster.
Mephisto had ways to feed his vices
through use of the government devices:
simply took one hallucination out,
and put himself in, with rubbish to spout.

12

Screen Resurrections

P uck found himself in a panorama
of dulled senses in a psych-ward drama.
His body would obey no mind-command,
and each sense drifted like a dune of sand.
The frustration of not being able
to skip free and be invulnerable
grew in his mind, and was only made worse
when he thought of the dangers, like a curse,
from the screen which channeled Iabud's show
as scripted and arranged by Mephisto;
whose corporate enemies had mages
for their own subliminal messages,
and Puck was caught between their battle-lines,
as each tried to snare with image designs.
Ricky Rodent was like Rome's religion
that adapted to each conquered region.
When ancient Rome fell, Catholics arose,
adopting many of the pagans' shows;
thus, there was hope when Ricky falls
a system would heed the audience calls
and there will be something to build on
for a body's true resurrection dawn,
instead of just sequels displayed on screens,
with casinos and sports for credit liens.

Ted, who sat next to Puck, smiled and rated
each show as turd or sophisticated.
In denial of critiques, Puck shook his head,
but could not shut-up the patient who said:
"Minerals, water, electricity,
and air are required for human's ditty.
The song of ripping out Earth's minerals,
with electricity rewiring skulls,
and polluted water and smog-filled air
are done to build a safe protected lair
to learn hymns of a Nirvana dude's bray,
which teaches that everybody is gay.
I have done my time in education,
and watched it become a degradation;
such as a Shakespeare porn version to teach
A Fellow and His Whore from Venice Beach.
They manufacture tolerance, love, hate
to gain rewards of what they imitate.
I cannot take it with me, and a cheat
can take it away, but revenge is sweet,
until the torch of wrath's vengeful cinder
scorches the world's tree to ashy tinder.
It hurts finances to teach that lesson,
so 'tis replaced by synthetic reason.
We are taught machines get vengeance for us,
so we work to build a credit surplus.
Existence is vows of work fealties
to buy proxy-lives through celebrities;
we all get the messiahs we deserve:
some get drunk, some lash-out, some think they serve.
Fictional revenge is purchased and staged,
so we feel catharsis and not encaged.
But what of it? The reason for most wars
is fiction skewering through people's cores:
the machine of the gods in each nation
consumes stages and imagination."

As Ted droned on, a nurse approached the pair,
and waved a hand in front of Puck's glazed stare.
She said: "You have a captive audience
to your views of political science.
Perhaps some of it seeps into his brain,
to become a disciple of your reign."
The nurse snapped her fingers close to Puck's ear,
smiled at his blank gaze and said to his peer:
"Between you and television 'tis sad
his subconscious fights over each new fad
that twines and warps, as he seeks to buy out,
or a peaceful means to resolve your bout
with all the screens you wage battle against,
recruiting believers who are incensed
they are pawns to be manipulated
by powers that keep them snared as fated,
and hope you will lead them beyond it all
in talks of new gods and the ride of Saul.
Somewhere in his brain, he may think his time
has come to evolve beyond murk and slime.
He might have created a great vision
in his skull, which has detailed precision.
Well, we teach substance abusers require
a Higher Power for the soul's empire.
You probably do not do more damage
than television's synthetic image,
so carry on, and if he shows a life
that stirs and awakes, call me from the strife
we have with Molly Mac on her ration
of nightly doses of medication.
I do not know why the hospital staff
thinks group-counseling is more than a laugh:
when crazy folks try to cure each other,
their weird insights make me say 'Why bother?'
But I have student loans I have to pay,
so if I do not heed what you all say,

nor take my duty too seriously,
I stay happy with how curiously
we work to adjust psyches to the screens
which sell new and improved satori scenes.
They fight his inner-beatific view
you help shape be unscientific stew."
Her small elfin face had highways of guile,
which brightened into a mischievous smile.
Ted was jealous and did not like the imp
who botched and ridiculed his plans to primp
Puck as an acolyte for Ted's belief,
an easy recruit washed up on life's reef.
She winked at Ted's envy and skipped away,
taking with her a medication tray.
Ted was about to go on with his speech
of how the health-staff was a psychic-leech,
as in old days when they bled a patient
to drain bad blood like weird voodoo would vent,
and that one could not be free of the Hells
by group-discussion or black magic spells;
one had to have belief in truth and guides
who knew the way to where honor abides.
But Ted was interrupted by a lass,
Nina Panlilla, whom Ted thought was crass.
She smacked bubble-gum and burped soda pop,
and her hair was a dyed green and blue mop.
Her informal manner was agony
to Ted and his raging misogyny.
She carried a pillow she sat upon,
an anorexic like a starving fawn
who lost her mother and could not forage
for herself through the brambles of life's stage.
Diet soda pop and sugar-free gum
was her calorie-counting menu sum.
Ted tried to dismiss all that went before,
and the present and future's looming lore.

Nina listened to proselyting Ted,
looked at drooling Puck, then giggled and said:
"You are worse than a commercial at night,
when one is asleep and puts up no fight
against the screen they dozed off in front of
promising a great product all shall love.
Energy used for self-satiation
of shallow image and reputation
seems an evil plot that Loki would hatch
to build identities for him to snatch.
Burning fumes on imaginary larks
'til matter is scorched and devils sing harks.
Some force helped keep him out of a sewer,
now you want him to be a scene-chewer."
Puck slowly explored his various parts,
amazed by works of the medical arts,
on which Nina and Ted voiced opinions
with fragmented identity minions,
who showed through shattered personalities
to become social liabilities,
who could not channel in the right station,
which made Puck think in fierce desperation:
I must be rid of these insanities,
caught between their embattled vanities.
Puck's mind began holding court to be rid
of shades and sprite spoilers haunting his grid:
divine or Hell blazes 'til it all fried,
a mini-Last Judgment which purified.
He saw a pin-point of light in his mind,
and thought it something to which he might bind
to start building a personality,
and revive from the psychic malady.
He found himself with a bearded cleric
in occulation as if walled by brick.
The ayatollah had challenged the rule
of Dabu, who turned sneaky and cruel

after he consulted astrologists
to discern the future from starry mists.
The bearded cleric refused to anoint
Dabu's son as chief-minister for joint
control of the nation, so the clergy
could not exploit the trade of energy.
The ayatollah counted beads as Puck
also muttered intricate prayers for luck.
The cleric had died by suspicious means,
and as a holy patriot who gleans
wheat from chaff, he made movements with his lips,
savoring tastes of the apocalypse
as the head of the communal effort,
which staged unveilings as the last resort.
The ayatollah had studied science
when he was young, and used his defiance
against Sheik Dabu to further the burst
in atomic structures of the accursed.
The ayatollah had light to direct,
and the bubbled cell was used to protect
his psychic means of manipulation
for vengeance to purify his nation
as a devout believer whom could aim
the wrath of the angels at those to blame.
The cleric looked at Puck's red steaming eyes,
and thought him a pawn to help win the prize
in games of faith and political chess:
even the wicked can serve the righteous,
like Dabu was overthrown by bad jinn,
who in turn must be usurped to purge sin.
Puck realized he needed a belief
in the Soma Wars which had brought him grief.
He had dosed the covert agent to see
things that were not there, then Puck paid the fee
of karmic levers when hospital staff
dosed him so he could neither cry nor laugh.

He needed order beyond the intent
of the atom god's micro-management.
New orders were rising with their own faiths,
using sundry Somas to recruit wraiths,
like Pharaoh Akhenaton and his one god,
Aton, who began Adonai's seed-pod
with dark energy between the protons,
the nucleus, and spinning electrons,
which formed Adam's contrarian natures,
now controlled by artificial sutures.
Each Quarter tried holding back Soma sprites
from inducing woes through artistic rites.
Meanwhile, Sistah, on the Yankee West Coast
was viewing video she would not post
as a preview until she could edit
the scene she watched, which might have some merit.
There had to be a way to blame white folks,
and get them to invest, and then the jokes
would be on the honkies who called it art,
and even teach it at their college mart.
They had so much wealth, they bought anything,
even guilt pointed at them, so a sting
was part of their pleasure in a purchase,
while safely protected from the slum's mess.
The previous night, Sistah recorded
a long scene that was part of the sordid
life of the gangster-crew she was filming,
who wanted a dynasty like the Ming.
Only violence, or the threat of it,
could produce the new order run by wit,
as forty years of thug-era teaching
evolved to a less violent preaching.
The time of white rule was nearly finished,
and the structure relied on what they wished
instead of what they actually did,
which was live in screens, auctioned at a bid:

whether it was white Russians and their Trump,
or pointless games as an unconscious lump,
they paid to watch fantasies of their doom,
feeling protected so they would consume.
White men demonized each other for wealth,
and to guide the herds of females by stealth;
black men were forced to follow money's voice,
and vilify themselves through lack of choice.
The documentary she created
gave her hopes of being highly-rated,
and perhaps win her some movie awards
if submitted to the right screen-guild boards.
For some reason whites liked receiving scares,
so long as they were safe within their lairs.
She would help put the fear of god in them
by showing what was outside their system,
waiting for either legitimate roles
that rose above their history as proles,
or would descend on white society
to reap for rewards with no piety.
Sistah lingered on the borders of peace,
so was unsure if she could use the piece
of recording made the previous night,
because it went far beyond vengeful spite
and sank to an evil which could dismiss
Sistah from being thought a serious
film-maker who deserved fortune and fame
for the one-dimensional shows of blame.
Toucan had allowed her into his home
after recording his rapster poem.
He was a sub-lieutenant in the gang,
whose chief allowed filming as Toucan sang.
Hotspur, the chief, did not want personnel
filmed in acts of illegal buy and sell.
The only face to be shown was Toucan's,
and there were other strictures of the khan's.

While in the studio, she overheard
Toucan tell Hotspur that all was assured:
the gangsters sent to a Midwest city
had an enforcer who showed no pity.
When the public, which he would terrorize,
finally jailed him, he could colonize
the penal system, and when he got out
would have no thing to lose, so bash about
in crazy, violent criminal deeds
to sow in the city the gangsters' seeds.
Then, for his mother, Toucan rapped a song,
which proved he had a good heart all along.
They drove to his apartment where his crew's
sergeant informed Toucan of awful news.
Sistah filmed during the pimp-discussion
of a woman they bought from a Russian
mob who thought her a liability
because she had lost her ability
as a high-priced whore who had laughing charm,
but freaked on a client and done some harm
to his face, so she could not be trusted,
though kept her good looks for men who lusted
after the sort who were meretricious,
selling her form which was voluptuous.
Sistah kept to the fringes of the group,
who did not notice she filmed the gang's troop.
She wanted something spicy to enhance
the documentary, like vicious rants
displaying that they were forced to be mean,
and this would be a good climactic scene.
The whore was in a room tied to a bed,
where Toucan peered into, returned, and said:
"I told you to get her groomed for the street
to be just another paid piece of meat
by burning out all her back-talking sass,
not to stick a firecracker up her ass.

There goes a good money-maker who might
complain to a trigger-happy blue knight.
You say she called out for her dad and mom,
and is our stupid white slut Auntie Tom,
but what if she decides not to forgive
because her ass is blown-out like a sieve?
She was the one who your anger and vice
was worked out on as a lamb sacrifice.
What are we to do with the silly wench,
since the plans are fouled by your monkey-wrench?
Hotspur bought the whore with cash, no refund
for a half-dead white slut, shattered and stunned.
And you do it in my own apartment.
I should bury three of you in cement
to teach lessons to the rest of you fools.
She might have been one of our best drug-mules
when painted-up pretty and taught the trade.
Now tell me of the problems with the grade
of black tar we have been selling around.
About that whore, none of you make a sound,
because you morons messed up what I said,
and now I need to get another bed.
If I think about it, my rage will blow,
and one of you goofs shall have your blood flow."
Toucan's veined nose colored when he was told
the new black tar heroin being sold
was too potent and killed off customers
both in the city and the white slummers
who came to buy the drugs to party with,
but instead were reaped by a deadly scythe.
Spare-change spoke for the crew, who were ashamed,
and hoped for no harsh reprisals if blamed:
"None of my troop know how to cut the junk.
We should buy it refined, not in a hunk
of raw material that is too pure,
because buyers die when they take our cure,

which means there are more police on the hunt,
and the street-crews are taking that full brunt.
Half of my guys are on bond or in jail;
some may snitch, then we get the hammer's nail.
I need to recruit troops, or other crews
will move in as territory-war brews.
But what can I tell the prospects I want?
That our dope is a cop-magnet who haunt
each side of the street because the dope kills
people who pay for god-kissing smack thrills?
Why not buy a building where we refine
it after being trained in its design?
Either that or buy it already cut,
which we break down some more, because this rut
we are in leads to the morgue or prison.
Our own neighborhoods hate every person
in this room for dealing out deadly horse,
and revenge may be a matter of course;
or even worse, start snitching on our crews.
We sit on powder-kegs with a lit fuse.
A free turkey at the holiday-times
tossed to them will not stop their angry chimes.
Even the police are hot on our trails
due to overdoses linked to our sales."
Toucan: "I do not want to hear you sulk.
Hotspur will buy the heroin in bulk
until he has enough cash to expand,
and buy buildings to refine it like planned.
I will try to hire some professional
refiners this week to act as counsel.
If Hotspur does not want to pay them cash,
we can give percentages on the stash,
but for now do not sell any more dope,
no matter how the junkies whine and mope.
They will have to tough it out a few days,
or go elsewhere to chew their cud and graze.

Now what is this I hear of Tire-iron
being chased by the local cops' siren
because he did not pay his child-support?
Do you really want to go to court
and explain how you drive a fancy car
by selling large quantities of black tar?
Most likely, your slut did it out of spite,
so damnit do not put up a court-fight.
Just give the woman cash to tend your brat,
and I will make your brain signals go flat
if I ever hear more of this again,
because this discussion is not open.
I want no child-support fights or gene test
giving officials reason for conquest
by throwing all you dead-beat dads in jail.
Remember that the next time you chase tail.
We want to achieve an impunity
by strong support of the community.
It is not enough to just terrorize,
we have to offer rewards and a prize
so they have good reasons to stay loyal,
then we can reach positions more royal,
which we cannot do by having a slut
tied to my bed for minotaurs in rut."
Tire-iron: "I recognize her from porn.
She was hot stuff before she got all torn.
Her stage-name, at the time, was God's Girlfriend,
but now even It cannot help her mend.
I have to be truthful with you, Toucan,
they recorded the plowing of her lawn,
and did not bother wearing disguises.
I only inform so no surprises
come your way if officials trace her plight,
because it was posted on her web-site.
One of these idiots has her cell-phone,
probably pinging off a tower's tone

to be tracked to us and bring our demise,
because a fool thought her cell-phone a prize."
Toucan kept his cool and held out his hand,
saying as he gazed at each of the band:
"Give over the phone and get out of here.
Four of you stay put, including our peer
who has the phone and used it to record
the raping of the girlfriend of the lord.
Ah, Fang-face, it was you who filmed my place
being the site of a total disgrace.
And I see you left the phone on as well,
inviting the cops to your debauched Hell.
I should send both of you to human-trade,
but have no time before a police raid.
Get his weapons and tightly bind his wrists.
If he acts tough, do not be shy with fists.
Take him and the slut to a vacant lot,
and give each a deadly heroin shot.
Bullets are easier to trace than smack,
but burn all the clues to cover your track.
I broke contact with her web-site Facepage,
where you proved she has a diverse image.
Do not record making her soul a shade,
as we are not in the snuff-movie trade.
Dump the wiped phone next to her burnt body,
and do a good job, not half-ass shoddy.
Just what will you idiots think up next?
Ordering food-delivery by text,
then killing the pizza-guy for ten bucks?
Your brains are like slapped-about hockey pucks,
skittering round, going for quick small cash,
and when you get bill-rolls, you have to flash
the money about so people can see
that you are a big-time champ on a spree.
You complain that Hotspur does not pay well,
but cash seems to put you under a spell.

We are saving up to make things happen
you can be part of, or land in the pen.
We can buy legitimate protection,
but 'tis costly to win an election,
and get the city council on our side,
with police and covert agencies plied
by funds, which gives us more freedom to move
outside this narrow niche, stuck in a groove.
If you want to stay poor and on the streets,
just keep doing these idiotic feats,
and wind-up with a bullet in your head,
or doing life in prison until dead.
Remember society wants order,
and we can spread it across each border
to make it in our image to control,
but we need time to formulate our role.
'Tis one thing to colonize with some thugs,
but land deeds, gambling, not just whores and drugs
can be our future if we work and try
to be royal gangsters and not small-fry.
Owners of legitimate protection
pay to keep us in our dismal section,
partly to have the profits for themselves,
and because the psycho-dope you take delves
into thinking only of the minute,
which you believe spans through the infinite.
Our ambition is beyond street-peddling,
a dream that does not allow your meddling."
Toucan did not delve into his new pact
with a sport's star and his t-shirt contract
made at his plantation in Honduras,
where Toucan's troops kept workers in duress
making shirts with the picture of a crook
who would be in prison if his life's hook
had not been yanked out by a savage cop
in a drug-spree, fake money traffic stop;

resisting arrest and killed in action,
sports' shows displayed safe racial reaction:
players kneeled at the national anthem,
racial justice became a slogan's rhythm.
The military protected each game,
while riots in streets burned stores without shame.
Sistah knew from contacts and news annals
that the crew were serious criminals,
but as she watched the screen of Toucan's speech,
she hoped his evil means led to a breach
that widened into legitimate gains,
which could purify the past's misdeed stains.
Maybe she could mask Toucan's face and voice,
and edit so it seemed he had no choice
in ordering the deaths of the doomed pair
who violated his law-coded lair.
Any breakdown of needed discipline
would make the neighborhood a loony-bin.
Though it was harsh to enforce such edicts,
a show of honor was part of the mix.
Sistah knew some of it was a façade,
and fear was instilled as the gangsters' god.
Communities needed forms of worship,
and she wanted an angle she could slip
in the film concerning the local faiths,
not just programmed killers of cutting lathes,
but like Crusades, Jihads, and Jewish Bans,
which were viewed as part of god's culling plans.
Faith in an apocalyptic stallion
was like riding on smack, horse, heroin.
Perhaps she could discuss some donations
to the churches and communal stations,
which would give Toucan good publicity
among clerics of the inner-city
and the workers in the social programs,
who thought gangsters were dangerous flim-flams.

Her film could be seen as documenting
the spirit against the unrelenting
forces that oppressed to wretched despair,
but the spirit rose with money and prayer.
Even if the fortunes were ill-gotten,
they improved conditions which were rotten,
and would only get worse, 'til they burned down
their own living space in that part of town.
There was no point in blaming the teachers
of self-justifying as god's creatures,
for she knew that dogma and rejected
their hypocrisy for a selected
building of truth through image metaphors,
which sailed illusion-channels to new shores.
Illusions need no justification
as hobby, religion, or vocation.
She required no self-absolving of guilt
in backwaters of her mind blocked by silt.
The state of bliss she reached watching a screen
was interrupted by a vented spleen
on her locked door, which shook from angry pounds
her neighbors ignored as far backdrop sounds
that were tuned-away by appliances,
so Sistah was alone with her chances.
Her first thought was to call for the police,
but would lose street-credit, as her life's lease
depended on being able to blend
with the neighborhood cliques, which would defend
their own against the unbalanced justice
that sentenced them to prison Hell's like Dis.
She went to the door and leaned against it,
and was determined to display her grit.
She asked who raised the devil at her door,
her voice strong, though she quivered in her core.
What seemed Tire-iron's voice: "Unlock the latch,
you silly, stupid, worthless piece of snatch,

or I will break it down and drag you out,
and down the hall while you gush a blood spout.
I saw you filming us last night and thought
you had permission, but now you are caught."
So they planned a public execution,
which meant it was beyond taking caution
she usually showed when with the crews,
though she had lost good tales they bragged in spews,
but refused to allow her to record
due to the discretion of their gang's lord.
She was cornered and thought with frantic rage
she would not be a victim on Facepage
as a lesson to all at the web-site
that interference bought a heavy smite.
She wildly thought of sticky tar-babies
heroin caused like a case of rabies.
Threatening their cash-flow had got her stuck
like she personally attacked their muck.
She ran to grab her Brer Dope and project,
thinking it was too much work to be wrecked;
if she escaped, it also could be saved,
and at that moment the battered door caved.
Sistah had no weapons except her wile,
because she knew it would become her style
to use a gun at slight provocations,
or want to make her own instigations,
giving her a reason to hurt someone
to settle a score or have wicked fun.
They came through the door, yelling awful cries,
as she got the fire-stair window to rise,
though it left on her hand a small, deep cut
because the window had been painted shut.
She climbed down the iron-rungs in bare feet,
hoping a gangster was not on the street,
guarding the escape route she had taken.
Her head was clear but her body shaken,

nor did it want to follow her reason,
'til she forced her will upon its treason.
She reached the alley with a six-foot jump,
landing just outside a huge garbage dump.
She had no time to think of broken glass,
or the alley's fetid odor of gas
rising to join the smog of the city,
as her bare feet felt the pavement's gritty
unrefined surface, not to be reformed
'til Armageddon was staged and performed,
and garbage sites took on life as 'tis writ,
with the polluted smog as its spirit.
She did not think her life had been wasted,
delving to where innocence was basted
by those she thought never had good choices,
which was reflected in the harsh voices
chasing her through the dim, infernal woods,
who wanted to franchise their neighborhoods;
she, too, hoped the money-machine would hum,
lauding her work so she could leave the slum.
Now it was too dangerous to stay there,
and could only afford the subway fare
to the central interstate bus station
to get outside the gang's bordered nation.
She would not bring raze and ruin to friends
and family with no means for amends.
She pushed distractions aside as she ran
'til winded, then she could concoct a plan.
When clear of the gangsters' territory,
she sat on a bench to plot her story.
She was shaking with fright and exhaustion,
feet bloody from racing without caution;
her hands were cramped from holding her work tight:
hardware and software that earned her hate-spite,
which could easily turn to a death-knell
because of illusions under her spell

through editing and adding sundry acts,
none of which would display the entire facts.
In the city she could use the sources
of public libraries, and the courses
taken through social programs for poor folks,
which fueled her inspiration with stokes
that blazed to be free to film as desired,
and those hopes turned to chilly thoughts which fired
hard schemes to wrack Toucan with her vengeance
when she contacted her movie agents,
and might get from them a small cash advance,
or apply for fine art government grants.
Perhaps she could get her own apartment
through a friend in a welfare department.
Sistah had not seen Nanya for two years,
but they had once been close party-peers.
Nanya had married and settled in life,
helping the unfortunate deal with strife.
Sistah was still using dope and hard booze,
so she would have to work some kind of ruse.
Through her life, Sistah had been pigeon-holed
to play parts with how money had her roled,
being labeled and fitted to a glove.
Time to show the world what she was made of:
a virus sends people further into
worlds of illusion, more tempting than true,
and her work would be there, waiting for them
to reward her with wealth and own system.

13

Programming Free Will

Daniel Tines had survived the ghostly calls,
and landed in the city of Sioux Falls,
with a free life from the community
and a loose rein, but not impunity.
He sat at his desk, thinking of the saints,
and what was life without any complaints.
His body was aging with a few kinks,
that he did not think queried like a sphinx,
and try to decipher stories and plays
to plot networks of future poem lays.
He got what he wanted, and was happy
without the lachrymose or the sappy
emotional twists of vast highs and lows
he used to study to discern the flows.
He still loved golden Circe, whom he met,
the daughter of the sun, whose rays and net
sank so deep in minds they became consumed
in coveting gold, as the Fates had loomed.
When nature had been churned and gold exhumed,
fossil fuel was next, burning the past,
and it seemed future roads could not be cast.
Tines had been driven on by destiny,
though he thought he was more than a tiny

mote castaway, awash by Samsara,
life's deathly ocean upon the terra.
New gods and goddesses assumed their state,
investing in lives and real estate,
where they could form their herds as they so wished.
Steering satellites, they hunted and fished
for those they considered above human,
whom could be useful with a sword or pen.
Computers were asexual teachers
of body holes having the same features:
vaginas interchanged with an anus,
and student loans could buy that happiness.
Thus they only achieve diversity
when their image is in activity
through all versions, with rewards in each tale,
with more prizes due for the stories' sale.
An anus is reward and guide to them
through all the wastelands in every system,
until a Rama Reagan trickle-down
owns it all with one monopoly crown.
Yet Daniel Tines knew his own fallacies,
and began to write of hypocrisies.
Trapped behind a self-image, yet decree
I help fill the story for all to see
how life and the resurrection digest
gods and beasts to be reborn and much blessed.
Shall I write any more in abstract art,
yet still encourage the corporate start
of blending images with deities,
who are merely corrupt celebrities
with selfish stories like the ancient gods,
who controlled life like cultivated pods?
No image of Yaweh, except Adam,
but what is the Word? Who gives a goddamn?
Aum it away and reset each Quarter
in nature without the bricks and mortar.

Deny temptations in my very core
that people are merely a metaphor
of signs and symbols, like runes to be used
in manipulating all to be fused
as a contrary to monopolies,
yet like them, I want rewards I can seize.
Should I fight over someone's gambling debts,
including credit and stocks that reach depths?
Like Krishna killing everything in sight,
even his kin, to end an era's blight.
We must decide what kind of wars we want,
yet as always the past returns to haunt.
For god, kin, country, or corporation,
wars are passed to the next generation,
as Somas evolve, and the breeding rights
rearrange power for the Bardo Lights.
What is not taught by celebrity lords:
screen-wars give one-dimensional rewards.
To make what is left behind of no use
against those who flee, drain it of all juice.
Revenge upon the spiteful destruction
ensures all get dragged through the Void's suction.
My compelled written words are made to strive
against the new hieroglyphs who arrive
to take their place across the screen-planets,
yet my words are turned to scripts by their nets.
Dan Tines stopped writing and looked at the wall,
wondering if he made a judgment call,
and been found wanting in his self and work
by karmic levers nearly gone berserk.
His writing was more philosophical
as he watched the new gods' machine cycle.
Was he passing along what he had learned,
hoping that not all of it would be spurned?
It was hard to detect what he could game
for himself in a nation crazed for fame.

To survive, he used the last solutions,
and became fragments of institutions.
'Twould be folly to deny their impact
on his reason, which made a peaceful pact,
forming a democratic state of mind,
which fought against the corporate designed
means to form those more innocent than he,
directed through consumption for a fee.
He saw the old ways become villainized,
and watched new heroes carefully be sized
and fitted to programs like a Pavlov
rigging people's faith that heroes can solve
all problems through his/her empowerment.
Tines detached, watching energy misspent
craft the scapegoats for the hour or minute,
like apocalyptic nags with no bit
bashing round the world, pretending to be
righteous wrath nailing bad ones to a tree
that grew fruits of knowledge, both bad and good,
which was banned to those of a neighborhood,
who had been purged of all unpleasantries,
and strolled perfection with god as a breeze.
Yanks obsessed on sex as a trendy thrill,
and lacked any interest in free will;
one had to go along with current fads,
or risk wraths of corporate moms and dads,
who planted in the public hateful seeds
at hard-cases not buying into creeds.
The cesspool waste was like hogs in the mud
sexed-out until wild lust left their blood.
The piglets were domesticated food
to be possessed by Legion and his brood,
like a virus made a rich-poor schism
in need of a food-chain exorcism.
Tines puffed a cigarette with clean spirits.
Should he fight corporate mandates and writs?

Like the women of porn try to outdo
all their competitors in pulpy-stew,
so was Tines trying to out-demonize
in knowledge that was a curse and a prize?
It was difficult to let the future
be sustained by artificial nurture.
Writing was only synthetic symbols,
washing him to imaginary shoals.
Even hieroglyphs were more pertinent,
as images rearranged to invent
systems of special effects that could train
minds to obey what is put in their brain,
and perfection can be manufactured
through digit lights in the minds of the herd.
Like the ancient Greeks heeded the queer-call,
Daniel's beloved had been alcohol.
That love was with him through many a strife,
'til new god-consciousness entered his life.
He fulfilled then split from Shiva duties
as the age dawned of rising deities.
The writers' bequeathing would continue,
though its presentation changed its venue.
The hieroglyph forms throughout satellites
orbiting Earth may attract by its sights
aliens who desire to colonize
the planet as gods or lord of the flies.
For the image networks displayed levels
of the good in people and their devils,
and the aliens as wish-fulfillers
could wreck societies to build pillars
and civilizations to fit their make,
yet plant seeds of rebellion in a snake.
Some women desire their own creation
with self-reflecting domestication.
When life was over-organized and set,
they found ways to disengage from the net.

Dan Tines had walked away from many shows,
sometimes rebellious in a Shiva-pose.
When he was young, was allowed to be wild,
but cameras and screens had people styled
to perform for their conglomerate cause,
though some morons recorded breaking laws
as if they did something great and clever,
web-posting it, which would quickly sever
them from a reputation to be bought
if, while wearing the wrong image, were caught.
The lords of the computers took their fee
from people to pose as the true and free.
Tines was half-civilized in mind and soul,
and his habits were no longer feral;
though he trusted his senses and instincts,
he put most of his faith into god-links,
like Thomas Aquinas reasoned about,
which led to Atman by indirect route.
Though Dan's body aged, and was somewhat stiff,
he did not want to be a hieroglyph
posing in a celebrity's story,
or a cameo in films turned gory.
Others might want to gain that ambition,
as scribes trolled web-sites, lost in attrition,
for dialogue, plots, and versions of tales
they can plagiarize for their own screen sales,
then accept awards in ceremonies,
where the audience becomes the phonies
whose work was stolen, and yet they applaud,
feeling they too receive a gracious laud;
yet wonder why their elected elite
steal and slowly compose a monarch's seat.
Secret code lords ran the economy,
and sneered at work of physiognomy.
When existence is chartered destinies,
those 'tis built on suffer harsh agonies,

whose only prize is watching the rewards
of those manipulating buddhi-cords.
Trends now have homophobia outlawed,
while queers bitch their own as uncool or flawed.
Dan Tines and booze parted without rancor:
it did not tempt, nor did he hate liquor.
His beloved alcohol helped save his wit
from the dullness the web-site stories knit,
with updated versions and oracles
which interpret everyone's fad cycles.
Alcohol and respect for Will Shakespeare
saved Tines from a professorship career,
because self-sabotage gave him a pass
on showing movies to a sleeping class.
He had not felt any white privilege
taking out huge loans to attend college,
paying white professors to learn that tales
must be retold to demonize white males.
His story-lines were judged an evil blight,
and Social Darwinism had the right
to crush tales like other cultures had been
since Ganesh used writing to enlighten
the fights to continue one's story-line,
and Dan got caught in their spirits' design.
Disabled by the ghosts' visions and moans,
he did not have to pay his student loans.
So Tines had a free life, and made the most
of watching a rising communion Host.
He disliked the way the world's doom was staged,
so had his own version written and paged.
Tines thought himself too old for adventures,
so became a voyeur to Yote's wild stirs,
and perhaps send him some of Dan's visions
which would require Yote to make decisions
on being a paradigm of humor,
yet beyond life as a fixed metaphor.

Dan Tines peered into Yote's rascality,
and saw wastelands of sex variety.
Tines detached from the incredible stream,
nor swam against rapids to spawn a dream.
All the species seemed in food-chain turmoil,
and the serpent wrapped round Earth in its coil
appeared to be in a great agony
of ecstatic raptures beyond money.
It was truly beautiful to behold
everyone free from a domestic-fold.
The climax exploded to colored lights,
then battles began for best breeding-rights.
A new lady of Nature worked her webs,
while Iktomi funneled climactic ebbs,
blending the Lady's work and artifice
for lingoes and numbers that were precise,
yet open-ended for no entropy
of tales' metered rhyme or a vast strophe.
Tines saw Yote split from Prince Rama, whose quest
would stabilize a region through conquest,
yet further a questionable gene-tag
because a shape-shifter, like a chief-stag,
stole Rama's woman as a wife-hostage,
so mixed songs were an heirloom of the stage.
Writing on a mental-ward, Donatien
Marquis de Sade becomes the god Dantin,
then matched with an elephant head, Ganesh
formed a tale that trapped Vishnu in its mesh:
begotten, virgin births, and pedigrees
made a self-genocidal clans' decrees.
Who can an imitative species blame
when taught to proxy-live for wealth and fame?
Yaweh's image made for obedience
helps create freedom-fighters at each sense.
Contraries in atoms always spinning
shaped the will to networks of pure sinning

when oppressive decrees are unjust laws
that pretend to come from the Causeless Cause.
Tines saw Yote thought those were greed-driven stars,
so avoided visions of oil-run cars.
The public's consciousness was lured and caught
by a machine's corrupt cognitive thought,
like Rama Ron's lost memory cult-songs
critiqued by Charles Manson-types over bongs
to franchise ape-mimic societies
that killed for one-dimension pieties,
which had democracy fall from high marks,
steered by global corporate oligarchs.
The audience watched fiction shows on screens
of the greatness of having kings and queens,
like the fad swept Israel to appoint
a king, as other realms had gods anoint.
Coyote was learning his own verses
with the Soma plant's blessings and curses.
Karl Berry joined Tines and watched Yote's journey
as if at a spectator sport tourney.
Tines had used Karl Berry's networks before,
and realized that Karl's Iktomi lore
had spread out and was ceaselessly written
from the first Big Bang to atoms bitten
into small pieces by technology,
gathered through webs in Karl's anthology.
The two smiled at each other in the night;
Tines passed to Iktomi the *Christos* light.
Though Karl disliked Dan's homophobic traits,
because Karl enjoyed some in-between states,
he accepted the light as rightful dues,
and proudly watched Yote, that poor sucker, choose,
while in an unguarded frame of madness,
some sort of order in his mind's duress.
Yote tried to concentrate on a female
who could inspire him through his tearful trail.

While Iktomi thought himself as the Word,
Yote followed the song of a desert bird,
who sang in a gnarled eucalyptus tree,
being no judge of Yote with a decree.
Yote cocked his head and listened to the tune
that went beyond the wasteland of the moon.
There was so much life and joy to be found,
even shifting sand was a lovely sound.
His mind revolved from darkness to solar,
with no boundaries at either polar.
The white's job was to build it up with blacks,
then tear it all down with gut-wrenching wracks.
Some believed the lord wanted it that way,
and so arranged it, demanding high-pay.
There had to be some kind of renewal
from the gluttony which never seemed full.
Levity ordered each vain, dancing mote,
and Gravity reformed the elder Yote,
so Coyote would dance between the two,
staying balanced in life that could renew.
Yote realized during his waking dreams
that there were many ways to gather seams,
looming it together to control fate,
and choose one's own creatures of patterned state.
The new Lady Nature slowly arose,
with her own singers and writers of prose
and poetry that she often guided,
who fought each other when she decided
she wanted a champion of the arts,
which included war in contrary hearts.
Then the winners set up metal icons
to the reforming arts of the new dawns.
Thus it was built-up until invaders
came to the territory as raiders,
who melted the idols to take the shapes
of their own champions, evolved from apes.

Digits run nations, symbolize gene-traits,
but numbers are not first principle states.
The ever-changing face of the heroes
in successive cultures became zeros
to cultures with faith in digital forms,
and Nature's ruined shape threatened death-storms,
as all of her champions were replaced
by those controlling the networks that laced
everyone in digit screen satellites,
controlling the Bardos as lords of lights;
with their own chosen people they select
those whom none in their right mind would elect.
The champions through the fake dimensions
help degrade the people's comprehensions.
Those who retaliate are put to shame,
and a god is slowly crafted to blame,
whose mold of minerals taken from Earth
becomes a wealthy symbol of high-berth
as reward for acting throughout Earth's scenes
to a resurrection beyond all screens,
unveiling a curtain of what they are:
a scorching fire to burn Earth to a char.
Yote blinked: Vengeance is to blame for their lot
when karmic controlling levers are bought.
Yet alone and unprotected, Yote feared
the stalking monsters who watched him and leered
hungrily to game Yote for their own use,
so he swore fealty to Nature's ruse,
but saw in her web-fate, that was open,
he would be the chief of her button-men.
Yote disliked his defenses being dropped,
not even for her, who had his thoughts lopped,
so he raced to Barf Bardos to get out
the Somatic plant in a retching gout.
Thus he rearranged atoms as they burst,
like forming an Aton who blessed and cursed

with laws impossible for all to serve,
so some split away, widening the curve;
thus the cycles did not feed on themselves,
and the poor could rise to the freer shelves.
The punishments for any backslider
had Yote want the cycles to spread wider.
People demanded things they recognized,
with their own images fitted and sized.
Songs collided, warping the tuned order,
evolving hymns to a god-emperor.
Into life's deathly ocean all would drown
when war, disease, and madness wore the crown,
with the bodies from famine as its throne,
and people were taught to serve as a drone.
At the edge of vast orbits that rippled,
there came a foe whose logic was crippled.
Yote had no artificial weapons' lore,
as he backed from the face which seemed to soar
from the sky, to gaze at him unblinking,
refusing the wide cycles of linking.
It seemed right some Yanks' narcissistic chase
was guided by a dyed, hideous face
tempted to bring perfection to the Earth
through its resources to make empty dearth.
Yote snarled at the monster's assumed seamed face,
nor would Yote serve as its fortified base.
Self-sabotage might be one of Yote's quirks,
but at least it was his own style of works.
The unity for protection became
a diverse program of cultural shame
for those who did not flow with current trends,
investing to support corporate ends.
The global economy was Mammon,
the god of wealth, who would strike through famine
by controlling agriculture and land;
Yote was not scared to bite the feeding hand.

He had dealt with traps in his ancient mind,
and chose the broad cycles being designed.
The face was an unrelenting spectre,
saying that Yote was a god-defector.
The face continued to have Yote harassed,
and he backed away, though not embarrassed
by charges of treason to any god
of the Earth or beamed from a spaceship's pod.
Yote's breeding attempt was a disaster,
but he refused to serve any master,
though tempting phantoms emerged from the face,
and Yote was promised an eternal race.
They would survive each version of worships
that culled the stage for the apocalypse.
Yote hated waging war in global spews
to enforce one's own Armageddon views.
Trophies held little interest for Yote:
good senses, strong teeth, and a fine pelt-coat
were all Yote demanded, at least for now,
so for a promised prize, Yote took no vow
of servitude, which he thought a disgrace.
He would find his own beatific grace,
and if she led him on a long, wild hunt,
their pups would be free, none of them a runt;
for the journey would strengthen Yote's fiber,
which would be no weak, digital cypher.
Yote watched the spectre's face plunge to a void,
and Yote was glad the face was paranoid.
It feared the blessing Coyote had received
in choosing free will's path, which he believed
went beyond the artificial cycles
that connected the twine of rewired skulls,
preparing shows, from which Yote had escaped,
to adopt identities that were shaped
by the corporate personalities,
to which people swore their life loyalties.

'Twas better than being a void essence,
and were protected by the network fence.
As young Coyote watched the spinning lives
tailing after the face in hard nosedives,
switching like Proteus through characters,
Yote learned lessons from shape-shifting actors.
He could play some roles and get the rewards
without having to bow down to their lords.
The prizes would not be a gilt package,
formed to connect the consumers' steerage;
the taste would be gamey, not high-rated
among those over-domesticated.
Yote could not keep his free will if he tried
to collect other's will and have them plied
in an orchestra of his conduction,
'til they spun in the Void's awful suction.
As the cyclones of actors reached their peaks,
Yote quit studying the sundry techniques,
and watched them rip like funnel-clouds of wrath
through eco-systems in a gnawing path.
Their limited ability to choose
roles that did not shift from a trendy-fuse
kept them in turmoil of self-sabotage
they hoped to avoid in their next voyage
of personality-switching, when drained
resources and rewards left the Earth stained.
Yote thought the cycles to traps were too small,
and brief elation was artificial.
He chose the bigger cycles to study,
beyond the Void's appetite for putty
to warp in its entropy-like image,
that self-fulfilled a prophesying mage.
The broader cycles would be eclectic,
with Thunderbirds making life electric;
the corded wires would be instinctual,
Nature supplying food-chain's victual.

The canyon between the Void and the next
cycle slowly evolved without a text
which assigned creatures to a hungry cast
as a civilized hierarchy caste.
The crimson Thunderbirds' songs rang voices
that led to mouth-like uterus choices
of embodiment hums in harmony,
and its discord was not over money.
They fought those who sought to micro-manage
to a trivial oblivion stage
of vengeful high-technology gossip,
which formed deceitful idols to worship.
Some thought scapegoat religions were to blame,
and set to smite them towards humble shame.
Money-changed coins, thieved by Christ the sinner,
bought bread and wine for his final dinner.
Forgiveness and trust are quite separate,
and when the command-chain is a thug-het
that forces servitude for lasting peace,
then rebels may slice out a bigger piece.
Gold scarabs evolved from elephant-dung
to teach the value of wealth to the young,
who spring from scurvy-mineral waters
to fight for heirlooms as sons and daughters,
and wealth's control of fertile sundry breeds,
and beakers for extinct or sterile seeds.
Whose turn is it to complain with a boast
their chosen people have suffered the most,
with a digital screen resurrection
because defiled Earth was sold at auction?
Mutants formed by Puck's dropsy solution
are minor to those bred by pollution.
Yote had tried an evolution short-cut,
and felt like a confused, mean, hybrid mutt.
New elder deities returned with fire,
which the world's voices summoned by its choir.

Young Yote hoped he had avoided service
so he and timeless others could gain bliss.
They charted no course at set times for shows,
nor adopted the current trendy pose.
Their schedules stayed as open-ended lives,
not auctioned programs in computer hives.
Yote did not even want to serve freedom,
though thought his tales would keep beat to a drum.
His feral pride refused to see the curve
of Nature unveiling how creatures serve.
She had stepped-in to take her new web-nest,
and collected males to sort out the best.
Yote scampered across the desert sand dunes,
while she wove tale-threads like the ancient runes,
with mixed new designs that were synthetic,
and timeless others beyond a relic.
She thought Yote could span the contrary loom,
but had to trap him to shape molds to groom,
which would not be as fierce as Gravity's
warping old Yote with harsh severities.
Coyote would be more fun than the new
Rama who changed from old Yote to Vishnu.
Nature liked some artificial choices,
but she preferred to influence voices
of those she felt she could make something of,
like Yaweh reflecting Its dearest love,
though their disparate ideas of laws
only reconciled in the Causeless Cause.
She thought over-domesticating breeds
required some free will sowing of wild seeds,
or they would not be able to survive,
except through what a tyrant might contrive.
Yote's place was in service to help evolve
creatures whose stories made the stars revolve,
'til the celebrities became masters,
then Yote would scatter stars through disasters.

Seeing this, Nature accepted the task,
and took a strong sip from her whiskey flask.
She wanted to dim some of the vast sights,
or she would lose herself among the lights.
The once benevolent gods of systems
turned wrathful in fear of losing faith-stems
which connected them to their believers,
whose evolving reached the new achievers.
Envy and spite became a rising tide
among the falling deities who tried
keeping faiths enraged with stupidity,
promising gifts to feed cupidity.
Yet many saw the stories were replete
with vacuous fury that would delete
the past that gave humans hope and trouble,
and future life would be in a bubble
where dignity and honor meant serving
a master-switch that was undeserving,
with workers farmed-out like a puppy-mill,
and the rewards being a dull screen-thrill.
Nature believed she could rearrange sites,
and inspire battle for clean water-rights.
Though she did not desire feast or famine,
she knew she might go to extremes to win.
What of that? Everyone else did the same;
winners told the tales, losers had the shame.
Coyote was something to build new dawns,
with stronger loyalty than dogs or pawns.
She would have to offer him some prizes,
which were like Pandora Box surprises
that released an energy of mixture,
which Coyote could use as a trickster.
He would be caught in those snares, without glee;
such happened to all eventually.
At least there would be hope in those fetters,
then Yote could have fun scattering letters.

'Twas that or Earth's resources, burnt to chars,
has smog block celebrities' hungry stars,
who thought they guided like zodiac signs,
and were worth their gobbling for brilliant shines.
She projected her feminine mystique,
and heard Coyote give a yapping squeak
as he chased the vision across the sand.
Nature thought: That was easier than planned.
Now I must turn my attention to chores
of sizing up my worst competitors
tugging at my loom to work devilry
in trying to weave the world's destiny.
When I get the fibers to unravel
at slave sweatshops where they make apparel
designs at the demigods' plantations,
then they shall face some harsh revolutions.
Thus ends unnatural looming of fates,
and the costume fashion industry states.
No longer imitators in disguise
of celebrities, consciousness will rise.
So Nature thought, as she sipped some whisky,
which scarred her mind's doors like a wrong-notched key.
She felt hot, then a chill ran through her bones,
and she struggled to straighten the loom koans,
that became a bizarre puzzling riddle,
which she strummed like an out-of-tune fiddle.
She continued to pull cords like a net,
feeling lonely and wanting a nice pet
she could groom and place her image into,
like Circe tamed Odysseus's crew.
Nature tried to fish out of Samsara
the soul of a being on the terra.
Coyote was lost chasing female signs,
so Nature read the poems of Dan Tines,
and snatched-up one of his most friendly ghosts,
elephant-head Ganesh, the scribe of hosts,

who was made by nature as well as art
that was natural, and a place to start
for her in weaving stories on her loom
to survive the corporate judgment's doom.

14

Fighting Over Ways to Die

Yote would not give his freedom nor relent
to shades wanting to be filled with content.
Though it was a means of collecting tales
through various zones with their Soma grails,
it meant fighting the shades' synthetic guide
who promised wealthy havens to abide
in safety and comfort from enraged hordes,
whom should be controlled by every zones' lords
working in collusion like arch-angels,
and contrary souls cast out in wrangles
to Hellish pits like a Dantean cull,
that were religious or political.
For Jesus promised followers world strife
would be rewarded with an afterlife
based on wealthy people's gardens of bliss,
and naysayers were thrown to the abyss,
where resources lit their tormented fuse
contrary to Heaven's energy use.
Other gods and prophets promised the same
to keep pace with foes in the rewards' game.
Yote's short life was on the periphery
of psychic round-ups, and wished to stay free,
though tempted by a messianic role,
where even capricious whims had control

over consciousness that sought to avoid
the purchased karmic wasteland of the Void.
So Yote retired from lessons of the Beast,
which coded people to famine or feast.
Tines watched Yote become a visionary,
like Browning's Sordello, who might tarry
in a forest, shaping a lotus land,
while others battled for the rule they planned.
Yote would leave it to a Dante's war-muse
to give political and dogma news,
nor be drawn in like a sad Sordello:
rustic idylls turned didactic bellow.
Who had the more unrealistic view,
with armies that were a murderous crew
to enforce their own fantasies of faith
to unmake or crush Yote's favorite wraith?
The prickly cacti Yote thought his mistress,
like Apollo and Daphne's love-distress,
would be deflowered by vicious winners,
and metamorphosis them from sinners.
Was it wrong to get lost in poppy's myth,
rather than reaped by third-dimension's scythe?
Yet the artificial sights' invasion
proved they could warp a natural vision.
If Soma could not be free of such kinks,
then Yote would have to make his own mind-links.
He laid under the cactus, its arms raised
as if in surrender, lost and amazed:
trapped between warring hallucinations,
and vain promises from incantations.
Dan felt guilt about the greedy designs
that stranded Yote on the stories' frontlines.
Dan saw mighty collapses in his day;
destiny had sent more than one his way.
He was spurned by parent corporations,
so became a state-ward for his rations.

Like forcing Natives to take bitter pills,
while ripping guts from the sacred Black Hills
to move dirt around in mineral blocks,
burying gold in Kentucky, Fort Knox,
and tubs of nuclear radiation
were dumped on a Native reservation.
So El Dorado changed its capitol,
as did means of exchange and capital.
Electronic funds guiding people's lives
has them scared to leave their synthetic hives.
Tines had studied free will, yet the abstract
was always easier than the true act,
which could seem to spin forth pointless results
that were reformed into popular cults.
Yet what could Dan Tines do, for Yote must face
the repercussions of the spirits' grace
thrilled by messiah roles Yote attempted,
but not lured by what the monster tempted.
Dan Tines empathized with Yote's exhaustion,
but Tines vanished again, heeding caution.
Karl Berry felt the void left by Daniel,
and Karl had no guidebook or manual
in how to protect Yote, except by songs;
and as Karl thought that, the ancient ghost throngs
collected around Yote and sang a hymn,
and Karl was convinced they all obeyed him.
When he tried to direct their healing tunes,
a chasm opened that churned forth the runes
which Karl had tried to write as the verses
of his pre-creation universes.
His soul was humbled by the sensation
of his work as a poor imitation.
Karl saw Lady Nature was out of touch:
one drink was not enough, and yet too much.
She knew her rising power was at hand,
yet there were things far beyond her command.

Vishnu was returning from his voyage,
and she wanted to snare him as a sage.
But he was sly and more tricky than Yote,
making structures that left her with no vote
or input beyond a breeding-program,
where she could be coddled and drink a dram
of Soma in a glorious city
if she bowed down to his authority.
New Lady Nature wanted her own mold,
not just icons of silver and smooth gold.
She wanted flesh, and would get it by stealth;
so thought of a daughter who desired wealth,
whom Vishnu had as an enduring mate,
while Lady Nature wove mixed webs of fate.
It was better than fighting over loot,
lost in fumes of resources that pollute;
all of which came from Lady Nature's stock,
then reformed as screen-images that mock
third-dimension denizens as the fools
serving hieroglyphs of those making rules.
New Lady Nature was ill from cheap booze,
and lost some status in a gambling ruse;
her chain-of-command once centered on food,
now 'twas based on an artificial mood
coerced to buy things with synthetic wealth,
which she would upset with her instincts' stealth.
Nature and artifice past certain means
unmans to birth all-devouring scenes,
becoming obsessed with performances
that are rarely worth one or two glances.
By wrecking nature, reason collapses,
and the soul goes in to demon lapses
that breeds a mixed polluted command-chain
of thinking you are god but quite insane,
while strumming the cerebral cortex
through buddhi-cords for a world searing hex.

The hollow self-image full of horror
spitefully becomes the world's destroyer.
Squirrel-girl returned from telling her boss
that some unknown power with wasteful dross
was invading the galaxy's bubble,
and seemed ambivalent to the rubble
left in its wake, chewing through every scene
like Milky Way infants who will not wean.
Her boss had nodded and looked deep in thought,
as if a trap had sprung and all were caught.
Squirrel-girl knew her boss did not worry
about a flotsam and jetsam flurry
that was part of daily work for free will,
which spun revolutions to laughter's thrill.
So his concern made her ponder the fit
the galaxy twirled in, as if some wit
prepared an unveiling of vast wonder
that showed them as a mere cosmic blunder,
a lesser spin-off of greater programs:
parodies full of self-important hams.
Her boss said: 'It comes to this decision.
You are now free to choose your own mission.
I did my best to gather free will's charge
fused with knowledge to expand and enlarge
beyond micro-managed obedience,
though I was tempted to control each sense
endowed to you fiends from a power-source,
and steer you towards an undefined course
that led from servitude's grueling grovel.
Now I will write a detective novel,
with fictional laws that enslave or free,
which may ripple waves through Samsara's bree,
so life's deathly ocean is not looted
by Ricky Rodent and his polluted
grabbing of all the various versions
of truth and fiction in spewed dispersions.

Whoever collects the most perspectives
rents proxy-lives to chosen electives;
the ambition to attain the lead role
keeps people investing, though a mere prole.
I do not need any further report:
I foresaw the new prepare to hold court
and judge us on whether they should join this
or spitefully smash for a catharsis.
You can tell the others, if you desire,
that I am no longer their liege and sire.
They can serve another if 'tis their choice,
or become renegades with their own voice.
I hoped there would be time to make a truce
with obedience that kept free will loose,
and not an over-organized structure,
but 'twill reform following its fracture.
That is for you and the others to choose;
my time is finished for tending your crews.'
Squirrel-girl thought: Well, 'tis time to scatter,
and hope free will seeds can grow in matter.
It must be bad if battle is fruitless,
and choices can no longer curse or bless.
My current shape needed no other prize:
money was not part of our enterprise.
I still have my freedom, so I will soar
through the channels for a last scenic tour.
Thus she found Yote, asleep but still twitching
from the throes of the Soma bewitching.
She landed near him and assumed a form
of a fresh yote lass wanting to get warm.
Her shape's lusty atoms whirled then grew firm,
but she thought her ghost was free when the term
was finished in laying with a wild mate,
so would enjoy a corporeal state.
She licked Yote's jaws and nibbled at his ears,
and he quickly roused from the induced fears.

Squirrel-girl had the appearance of youth,
but was an ancient spirit who had truth
locked inside her for her own creation,
which included rest and recreation.
She slowed Yote's fervid passion to a pace
which seemed to open all of Heaven's space.
Lady Nature was caught in her own looms,
while the two even harrowed Hellish fumes
that met with the network's sky for a mix;
Karl added their moves to his bag of tricks.
They collected resources and treasure,
'til Squirrel-girl was scared of the pleasure.
Their shape-shifting turmoiled through each network,
and she could not escape feeling berserk.
It went beyond tomes of love with prowess
and *The Book of the Dead*'s hateful caress.
She did not want to be a role-model
of love-making to peak at full-throttle.
Her form changed to an ancient succubus;
undeterred, Yote became an incubus.
She thought: He wants to bring in a star-child
from a galaxy gone nova and wild.
'Tis not a wise move to have a burden
during fall-out from new Hells and Eden.
We would be hunted to smash the old way,
nor could I rely on this mutt to stay
with us for protection to build a clan,
because he always ferments a new plan.
Thinking that, she gathered her strength and pushed
Yote away from her, and a vacuum whooshed
between them and they collapsed, exhausted,
each feeling like they had been accosted.
Yote was back in his familiar body,
but his consciousness was blear and spotty.
He felt like bragging a fantastic howl,
but his mind slipped as if draped by a cowl.

He was not the one who invented sex;
to think he did, might punish with a hex.
He should do something for the lass who brought
him knowledge of how love-battles are fought.
He slowly sat up and panted a bit;
his mouth was dry and could not work up spit.
Squirrel-girl staggered under the cactus,
thinking she had done more than a practice
of love-techniques, which the fiends did for sport
when bored or lusty like sailors at port.
Yote had entered her mind with snaring surge,
and she would have to find a cleansing purge.
Then she thought: I am also liable.
When did I want someone reliable?
Is it due to cosmic structure's changing,
losing my troop and our free will ranging?
Yet I want to keep my independence,
so why hook-up with a mook who is dense?
I do not like the feeling of capture
when a one-night stand becomes the rapture,
like some sort of Dante cosmology
invented for tantric doxology.
Old stars are part of constellation forms,
now hidden by smog and final firestorms,
so a new astronomy arises:
nova planets are pieces of guises
aligned to make sense of the universe,
like bears' and hunters' astrology verse.
Thus all are parts of awakening shapes,
some lost while trying fantasy escapes,
as bits of a constellation reflects
how a hunter's or bear's soul genuflects.
Squirrel-girl did not have one tailor-made
by star-gazers who thought her too low-grade.
Which was another reason to rebel
at the energy working a hex-spell.

The wildfires in California's regions
blocked Hollywood's stars with smoky legions;
now that Squirrel-girl was a free-agent,
she might find work with a rising regent
who kept her independent of shackles
tied to the stars' zodiac oracles.
As the sun began to rise, Yote limped off,
having wallowed in a sex-banquet trough.
He steered clear of the revelers' campsite,
who had fled Hollywood's wildfire storm blight,
but did not have the means to colonize
the desert with their ways to civilize.
Since theaters closed due to a virus,
they shared Armageddon's burnt papyrus,
like when the Black Plague closed Shakespeare's Globe scenes;
pageantries' image of smoke-mirror screens
shutting down would make Saint Augustine rile
as when Rome fell because its shows were vile.
Then the Catholics also turned to rot
when protecting pedophiles was their plot.
A new pageantries' oppression would form
that promised relief from the rerun storm.
Yote went up a sand-dune, then climbed a slope
in a weary fashion, too tired to lope.
Beyond slight knowledge of where he wandered
did not interest Yote, for he pondered
deeply the previous night on Soma,
and felt lucky to escape vast trauma.
Traces of the experience lingered,
as if red wrath stretched out, many-fingered
and groping for Yote's final surrender
to cosmic-stock of a credit lender.
Yote scratched around his body with a paw,
trying to ignore everything he saw:
compelled hollow horrorshows for each sect
that promised the screen-worlds will resurrect,

and buy all the versions of tales, then choose
the ones to sell to collect the most dues.
When all was owned by one corporate grid,
every perspective was taught as valid
if it helped spur on the economy
webbed by Ricky Rodent, not Iktomi.
Parent corporations, at all levels,
displayed foes' lineages as devils.
The chase for a trivial oblivion
through wastelands and commercials for Zion,
became a pointless and absurd pursuit
because the whimpering land bore no fruit;
this is what Yote howled at atop a cliff:
not at a bang, but empty hieroglyph.
Like Ragnorok formed by fortune-sellers,
currents of smoke pursued the revelers.
The sky was thick with a brown and gray mass,
and no network was left to let Yote pass.
Ah, how terrible when life's tasty fruits
were devoured by gods with false attributes.
Even worse was their vacuum of nothing
in a closed system where Yote had to sing
of frustrated despair after love-play
brought a clout on the head because his way
explored and connected what could be webbed
on Samsara's tide as existence ebbed.
Yet why would he desire life with a clan
instead of traveling without a plan?
There are more than enough creatures who think
they have a superior genome-link,
so why tinker to make perfect gene-traits
who fight to spread their monster race through states?
Yote was not a priest for celibacy,
and Squirrel-girl was sleek, fun, and racy,
but was already gone on her next move,
sliding through the airwaves to find a groove.

Perhaps she thought he was not good enough,
but Yote did not want to think of that guff.
They were both free, though it had been intense;
she wanted her own life's experience.
He would not begrudge her that, though felt sore
she had direction and could find a chore
to keep busy and not feel a besiege
to own or guide her by lady or liege.
She could serve independent productions,
as a modern virus formed screen-suctions
that drew people into isolated
bubbles to have their egos inflated.
Because screen lives have no consequences,
responsibility in sequences
has no place for good or evil displays,
so why not redesign Will Shakespeare's plays
to fit trendy perspectives as discerned
in forums where good credit can be earned?
Gaming it for rewards is a just Cause,
because screen lives do not have karmic laws;
then teach the lesson that it is all good,
if the law to obey is understood
and practiced for a benevolent grace,
which buys into everywhere and each face.
Asking for trust, the machine of the gods'
sell private information of our pods.
Credit companies sell retail listings
of purchasers to entertainment kings
and queens who quickly portray in the modes
the trendy items in people's brain-codes.
If Trump did not get a share of the cost,
he damned and outlawed it as anti-Faust.
So corporations paid Trump a tribute
to not be censored as Forbidden Fruit,
thus steered the forums to manipulate
consumers to an algorithm fate.

They would gladly punish Trump when time came,
yet censoring knowledge is the true shame.
Yote had no interest in the sections
being gathered or culled in collections.
Yet as he paced the ridge he felt hunted;
the dope made his wits fearful and blunted.
He thought: Hallucinations had me flee,
and I should not take it personally,
but when I view the looming webs they net,
'tis personal when one is the target.
It is best to stay out of a corner,
or I will become my own dead mourner.
Toward myself, I must be more callow,
and not invest in self-pity's wallow.
Their culture's technical complications
has people demand more faith-vacations:
paying for compelled sensitivity
of a show's fictional nativity,
with a yogi-brat birthed to steer a course
for the galaxies through use of a force.
Yote had tried the messianic approach,
complete with visions from the Soma poach.
Alone now, his head spun in a wide swirl:
had he hallucinated Squirrel-girl?
Breeding star-children for war seemed the verse
that sung and strummed cords of the universe.
It was all linked together and arranged
from the furthest stardust to where Yote ranged.
The ayatollah, in occulation
with lost Puck, felt a hearty elation.
Sheik Dabu was scared so bought Trump's favor,
which Ricky Rodent displayed for savor
by Americans used to taste-testing
as they ate in front of screens, while nesting
at comfortable regions selected
for their appetites to be protected.

The ayatollah read the omen signs,
which included Israel in designs
of conflagrations of blasting fireballs,
with civilians crying out their death-calls,
and praying for release beyond intent
of the global show by Ricky Rodent.
As Iabud fired Nari to burn,
the ayatollah would make his return,
taking with him his previous knowledge,
which would help him fulfill his vengeance pledge
on Sheik Dabu, who became a traitor,
upsetting balance to pose as greater
than religion or the laws of the land,
which the fist of god would restore as planned.
Civil war crushed some of Dabu's regions
that Mephisto had claimed with his legions.
The Yanks' delusion to fight all devils
came true as they partied on in revels,
hallucinating that war would bestow
stable profits by fighting Mephisto.
Yankee taxpayers funded Israel,
which used the money to buy souls in Hell,
otherwise known as Yank politicians,
who, like Doctor Faust, have great ambitions,
so their voters' armies and finances
are used for posing in righteous stances
for wars in a Muslim state like Iran,
which the Jews want destroyed with Yaweh's Ban.
When Yanks ring victory's chime, the won oil
is not granted them as rewards for toil,
but sold to Israel, for kickback bribes,
outdoing Jacob, father of their tribes.
Puck's roommate, the cleric, had other schemes
of doing god's will and bursting the seams
that corruption used to maintain order
on world-scale, overwhelming each border.

He believed evil could be forced to serve
good ends, but then evil had its own curve,
which meant when they had fulfilled their purpose,
they tortured the damned, gathered in surplus.
Thus, the Yanks celebrating through despair,
served the cleric's god towards good repair,
then would be culled out, and most of them doomed,
misled by images carefully groomed.
Puck watched the cleric sing incantations,
which seemed a good way to pass durations
of time while watching stars slowly collect,
and Puck did not mind the benign neglect
which put him in a peaceful, watching cell,
not knowing Mephisto's version of Hell
was trying to be manipulated
by Puck's roommate to serve an elated
apocalypse that the cleric would guide,
wherein Puck had enlisted on each side.
Eventually, his brain was a mess;
boredom led to feeling dull and anxious,
so Puck said: "Please, sir, let me in on this,
if you are preparing a soul death-kiss.
I know I should serve god before myself,
but what can one expect from a sprite-elf?
I have personal vengeance to attend,
and will serve your god if you tear and rend
my enemies with your glorious gift
in the Last Judgment of the final rift
between evil and those pure by god's grace.
Yet tell me first: is it only your race
and creed system this doom is applied to?
Because my vengeance aims outside that stew,
and I do not desire part of a chore
that denies hate satisfied in my core."
The cleric was busy with god's empire,
conjuring angels and beasts of wrath's fire,

ignoring Puck as a stray soul drawn in
the vortex of the war between the jinn.
He was of little use as a weapon,
or to sacrifice like a low-caste pawn.
Puck was annoyed by the ambivalence
shown his old sprite, not in adolescence,
or a catch-as-catch-can wandering ghost
who glommed to higher-degrees for a host.
Puck had self-respect and reputation
to be acknowledged in their shared station.
For some reason their stories were entwined,
so why not further what fortune designed?
Perhaps a simple mirage phantasm
that gave the cleric a haunting spasm
would make him more conducive to Puck's aim
of vengeance in the ayatollah's game.
Puck saw his former master, Oberon,
take life as the hunter the stars had drawn,
and pierce the lower sky with arrows' light
to terrify Earth with the angels' blight.
The old did not fight the newly arrived,
but smote the planet for a spite contrived
that if they could not have the Earthling's faiths,
no things would be left to feed the new wraiths.
Oberon or Orion, he would flay
the planet for Armageddon's display.
Puck watched the cruel hunt for denizens
whom had once been Oberon's citizens.
If the cleric could control Puck's old boss,
then Puck's dropsy was likely worthless sauce.
'Twas best to stay clear of this riled cleric,
until Puck conjured a more potent trick.
Oberon was clearing away his tracks
so he was not followed by vengeful packs
of those he smote while reigning as a lord,
nor leave anything for the rising horde

whose arrival signaled Oberon's end,
though did not realize that to offend
in such a way made his punishment worse:
vengeance is a coin in everyone's purse.
The satellite feeds were first to recoil
from the lightning bolt arrows' grim turmoil.
Those connected to electricity
through appliances in every city
at first received a tingling static jolt,
that increased with Oberon's arrows' volt.
Other constellations quickened to life,
trying to outdo each other in strife,
while the believers in astrology
speculated bets of doxology;
so as to profit from the stars' movements,
experts were on screens with urging comments
to get investors into their markets,
some of them backed by Mafia rackets.
When Gravity tried to control stars' style,
he found it was a bad job, not worthwhile.
The performance had demented humor
as threads spun crazily from fates' loomer.
Nova planets in each constellation
tried to gorge itself to satiation;
the solar systems fought in tearing rips,
spinning their true believers to eclipse
contrary suns by the planets' shadows,
and thus be the light that could preen and pose.
Planets collided into each other,
forcing their enemies' stars to smother.
Space was filled with asteroid-dust litter,
like Earth's remains after wars for glitter.
In-fighting between the stars reflected
the constellations' war as directed
by the cleric, who soon lost his controls
when outer-space tidal waves assumed roles,

like the neo-Vishnu washing from shores
of universal identity doors,
which opened with love's mischievous laugh,
releasing a new contrary work-staff.
Puck's node was like a batted about ball,
and he was willing to become a thrall
to a contestant to stop the beating,
as the cleric hollered they were cheating,
and were supposed to serve at his command,
channeling them with a sleight of his hand.
Many Earth spirits could not choose a side,
though enraptured by the new rising tide:
Samsara that shaped what people believed,
and too late the ayatollah perceived
the convulsive throes of old stars' twitching
empowered the new waves of bewitching.
Some did battle against the old stars' spite
wanting oblivion in a fire-fight
of a dance that was not choreographed,
like Shiva's when the world is sunk in graft,
and artificial coins become the means
to buy resurrected synthetic scenes,
formed by false prophets for Ricky Rodent's
rigged games of speculative investments,
including stars' sportswear made in sweat-shops,
like plantations owned slaves to pick the crops:
plastic and rayon replaced king cotton,
but old ways were not lost or forgotten.
The humming of the textile mill inspired
new movements among the workers, who fired
the building in a blaze seen from afar,
feeding on brand-name gear of a sport's star.
Similar occurrences seared the Earth,
for hatred was not a fuel in dearth.
Rebellion started on Samsara's boat,
and might climax with the antics of Yote.

Whose side would he take, if any at all?
There were many voices with luring call,
and representatives were a sly lot,
portraying themselves as having a plot
with compassion for humanity's part,
contrary to god's narcissistic art.
Their anti-god propaganda screen-fare
was something even Nazis did not dare,
though held grand sporting events to collect
people's consciousness of the faithful sect.
Empty arenas do not stop Yank sports,
as players live in anti-virus forts,
while screens reproduce all the tepid fares,
with subliminal messages, to lairs.
One-dimensional shades will fail to rule
when Nature's webs are freed from the threads' spool.
If a system's corruption is awful,
religions can make rebellion lawful.
To escape a land's misery, a chant
of: 'Islamic State of Iraq Levant'
howled when their army's dissolvent occurred
after George Bush Junior's troops had conquered,
and the natives had no security.
Much like Malcolm X met authority
while in prison, and became well-suited
to Black Muslims who groomed and recruited
the disenfranchised, pointing at scapegoats
living in Green Zones or castles with moats,
whose fairy tales and Plato Ideals
show rottenness when the screen-image peels.
Malcolm X taught to lay blame everywhere,
from whites, prophets, or for losing one's hair.
Like Mohammed's heirs, a breeding-program
split the Black Muslims like a hate pogrom.
Malcolm tried to invent his own chartered
religion that he and god had bartered.

Pope Malcolm was the executive chief
and the first martyr of his new belief.
A pimp like Charles Manson, both invented
dogma for those whom Heaven attended,
with varying theology levels:
blacks as sub-species or whites as devils.
Such are Hells born out of a prison fate,
and can be applied to the Iraq state.
The chief politician of Hollywood,
Rama Ron, led the stars against the brood
Ravana Charles gathered for revolutions
the government inspired with solutions
of psychedelic Soma for control
of military prisoners' doped soul,
which Ravana Charles used to inculcate
in others a frenzy of love and hate.
Rama Ron and Ravana Charles had those
they proxy-lived through to destroy their foes.
Later, as president, Rama Reagan
told insane lies while doped like a pagan.
Much of his country followed his drugged-whims,
loving oil and hating Iran Muslims.
James Brady, a talking head of office,
was brain-wrecked when a bullet went amiss
in Hinckley's shooting-spree at Rama Ron,
like Vishnu's skull was wounded by Ravan.
Protecting stars' oracles is a job
of numbered pictures planted in the mob.
Thus the *Odyssey* story was passed on
to the next greedy Yank generation,
tapping at screen-buttons as chimpanzees,
like Rama Ron trained Bonzo to earn fees.

15

Summing up the Parts

Mountain Berry awoke on her dad's couch,
which was too small, so she walked with a slouch
into the kitchen to make some coffee,
subconsciously thinking of where to flee,
or get a disposable job and rest
'til she recovered from the grueling test
of her mental and spirit faculties,
and invented some covenant treaties.
Along with Daisy, they burned down the roads
to a climax that altered Mountain's modes
at various levels, which had been served
a punishment course-banquet she deserved.
Discerning what was real or fiction
needed lubricating to stop friction
in the synapse of her fighting brain,
but alcohol might make her go insane.
She wanted something more reliable
than booze, which would make her incapable
of following the steady or sublime
and get free of that whirring Hell to climb
to Limbo or some Purgatory jobs,
by use of right keys at her mind's doorknobs.
She could gather again the accouterments,
and properly display her repentance

to society for pawning the stuff
they measured life by, 'til she had enough
money to purchase her most recent binge,
which made the doors of her mind-halls unhinge.
The warps in her body matched her mind's kinks;
she needed exercise and new thought-links.
She had worked at most of the franchises
to pay for her binging enterprises,
so her files on computer were world-wide:
'Do not rehire', so she would be denied.
As the brewing coffee began to perk,
she thought of asking her father for work
at the casino he invested in
through inheritance of adopted kin.
When Karl was four, he and his two siblings
had taken from their parents bad beatings,
and were put up for adoption to whites
when their tribe did not invoke legal rights
because there were no extended members
of clan not lost in alcohol embers.
Karl accepted they were responsible
enough to know it was impossible
for them to take in three children to raise,
but the whites' order of life was a maze,
forever in search of the great rewards
for being good, and prayers to the right lords
could be actualized at all work-sites
where hierarchies practiced ethic-rites.
Karl's siblings were too wild, so they were banned
from the safety of the chain-of-command.
Karl played his role, though his feelings were tense,
and received all of the inheritance.
His adopted kin dead, Karl's self-control
was like a gopher's in a foreign hole.
He went through a few meandering years,
trying to connect with some of his peers.

He went to prison and decided life
need not end with a mattress-spring shank-knife.
He invested in a casino-chain
after his felony was cleansed of stain
through a lawyer acquaintance who purchased,
free of charge, stock in *Blackbeard's Treasure Chest*.
Karl was not naïve, so 'twas no surprise
gambling in Sioux Falls had Mafia ties.
He paid for protection, gave them tribute,
and rented their gambling machines for loot.
He was currently in a bitter bind
since politely asked to join a designed
task to launder drug-money for a boss,
with Karl's account books redone to emboss
a gleaming fine display of large profits.
Though the offer did not make Karl throw fits,
he knew they could easily buy him out,
not being one of them and lacking clout;
or they would take Karl's business for their own,
using blackmail's essence with the seeds sown.
Or rig, at the same time, all their machines
to have giant pay-outs beyond the Karl's means.
Or simply burn down the establishment
rather than fit Karl with shoes of cement,
since there was no large body of water
for baptism as a gambling martyr.
A cornfield would be a more likely site
for Karl's burial due to gangster spite.
The mob could get Karl to do as they willed
if able to have John Kennedy killed
due to his brother persecuting them,
and loss of control in their game-system
in Cuba after Castro's rebellion,
and the heirloom of the swine invasion.
Romans were practiced in a gambling spin,
but the 'either' 'or' chances pricked Karl's skin.

They were serious criminals, whose means
were behind politics and legal scenes.
Since the legalization by the courts
for gambling in all states on sundry sports,
mobsters opened their books and recruited
soldiers for the street-jobs they were suited;
or hire dirt-work done by someone outside
so the media-forums would decide
the mobsters were not involved with the crime,
and some other thug would do prison-time.
Karl's competition made them capable
of evil, for he was expendable.
Gratuities were an easier plan
instead of robbed weekly by a crime clan.
The high-stakes had the mob families' greed
quickly grow with paranoia to feed
the desire to colonize vast regions,
and not be squeezed-out by other legions.
Like Guelph and Ghibelline wars of the past,
each wanted their own ruler, built to last.
Huge gambling slowed due to the pandemic,
which had branched through zones to be systemic;
while officials denied obvious facts,
refrigerated trucks with body-stacks
began to be part of the daily show,
because morgues were filled from the virus woe.
Mobs filled the streets, both pro and anti-Trump,
as if to bail poison with a bilge-sump
from the foundering ship of frustration
at the end of his administration.
Like a degenerate gambler who lost,
Trump failed to rig votes at taxpayers' cost
by trying to wreck the postal service
so the mail-in ballots would go amiss.
Eating a doughnut with her coffee-dram,
Mountain Berry watched some of the program.

Did it all come down to dollars and cents
in the way people had the world make sense?
Karl had tried to teach her some Christian lore,
but she found most of it a yawning bore;
the hierarchy of a faith's reason
caused rebellions through self-induced treason.
It was time to be domesticated,
or at least pretend it was so fated.
She flicked stations 'til she found a channel
where collected weirdos were a panel
debating Trump's refusing transition
of clout to Biden. One's odd position
was: "Trump plays for time, rallying cohorts
from mobsters to judges of sundry courts,
giving them plans to kill Biden and blame
Iran so Trump can start an oil-war game,
which Israel and Islamic allies
profit from like they fight The Lord of Flies.
Trump's congressional republican pals
will make sure Harris' career has death-knells
as vice president-elect of the Yanks,
so Trumps stays in power with the file and ranks.
Some criminals prefer that in four years,
after unrest settles and virus fears
have dissipated, then Trump can regain
the White House, or perhaps his son can reign
for profiteering to get up to speed
with global illicit deals to fill greed."
Mountain recalled the previous night's dream,
seeing a colored spray hit like a beam
of kaleidoscopes old Lady Nature,
which frightened and thrilled her with a rapture,
and she slowly slipped to death from her seat,
to an open maze that led to raw meat.
Gates slammed behind her, and her tiger's hide
would be skinned when it was time that she died.

The pelt was sold to one of the Brahmins
to sit on and meditate as a means
to enlightenment far beyond nature,
free from the cage of his mortal stature.
Satori was based on freedom from care,
but a tiger's pelt is a costly ware.
So predators had become ones to kill:
barnyard animals of a tiger-mill.
The hunters for enlightenment will seek
to have systems where they stay at the peak.
Mountain could not decide which paths to choose
because all communing did was confuse.
She felt micro-managed society
resented her self-chosen piety,
which was catch-as-catch-can experience
not based on money, dogma, or science.
Learning to think for oneself does not mean
subliminal messages from a screen.
She had men as partners for adventures,
and parted freely, without indentures.
Riding bikes through cities, sitting at parks
watching mated ducks swim with quacking harks.
Now she sat before a screen with no guide,
thinking Lady Nature would lose her hide.
Mountain wondered if she became too old
for burning down the trails, half-wild and bold.
She disliked the world seeming to narrow,
but her past was not a Hell to harrow
by any preachers or a messiah
reforming matter, which is called Maya.
She had read her horoscope every day
when she was a beggar and had to stay
at a homeless shelter, where newspapers
guided her to a job and next capers:
work advertisement for a hotel maid,
and road-advice so her star did not fade.

She had bounced back, and had fun with Leonard
riding the bike-trails until his fate whirred
him to the rez where his sister had died,
and his sorrow was so dark it denied
her the chance of being any comfort,
and she lost her partner in fun and sport.
When eighteen, Mountain had a miscarriage,
and after prayers, fertility's message
that she was not meant to be a breeder
had her tie her tubes against a seeder.
She wondered what her dad did in his room:
chasing after concurring faith and doom?
Why was she stuck around these crazed pursuits?
Then thought of her burned roads for tasty fruits.
Sleep deprived, Karl watched the birth of nations:
battling borders of hallucinations
that were seamless yet fought with enmities
for defined, fictional identities.
The struggles helped compose their story
of who they were through all of history.
Parent corporations tried to shepherd
the flocks to screens to gull minds with absurd
and vapid programming made by groomers
who steered the fated wires of consumers.
Like the Jesuits, they believed their job
would make the world better than the doorknob
to temptations' first principle knowledge
not found in numbers and beyond the pledge
to a corporation's chartered sworn oath
in the lies and myths invented for both
people and machines for a Golden Age
of profits like when Saturn was King Mage.
Karl discarded Iktomi's fated thread,
and saw a network which forever fed
on itself in cycles of hate and love,
wanting peace but ruled with an iron glove.

Dan Tines had passed the *Christos'* light to Karl,
which inspired a domesticated snarl
when he studied the ancient traditions
that fought against civilized oppressions,
which promised amenities and comforts
for obedience to judicial torts
from global corporations, which like Rome,
gave civil status in the empire's home.
The maze of walls Karl had built funneled him
to light beyond existence, never dim
and always forgiving to human shame
for needing a god to take all the blame.
Free will was crafted, yet also expunged
when people took that awesome leap and plunged
into a realm of faith and doubt's despair
to hide from the light in a darkened lair.
God did not work with traps, yet Karl was caught
in a presence that held him, and he thought:
Another Ganesha and Iktomi
will rise, but the favorite son is me.
Am I responsible for the mimics
who follow and stir a destiny mix?
Karl tried to groove the light for his freedom
out of the multitudes whose greedy sum
imitated him for the wealth promised
in a paradise beyond the Void's mist.
He hung, balanced between being a ward
of the Father and those wanting reward.
He could not go back to old Native songs,
as he competed to right awful wrongs
by god's other children, who gamed their zones,
playing dice, jeering his crucified moans.
His own pre-creation stories now wrote
him as a beloved, abandoned scapegoat.
He turned from the light's hovering mad glare:
he would take hostages and claim his share.

His name and work would be forced on natives,
spread through the world where dark ignorance lives.
Peasants who worked land owned by the elite
evolved in America a great feat:
credit and computers were now the fields
sharecroppers worked one-dimensional yields.
Corporate hybrid crops controlled the course
of food-energy at the seedlings' source.
Agrarian faiths and each four season
were replaced with artificial reason:
tales for farmers and fishermen were trite
compared to a nuclear atom's light.
Representing the *Christos'* flare to them,
Karl would bless his chosen; the rest, condemn.
Thinning herds to favorites was a chore
for a king and shepherd's passed along lore;
and now people were easy to corral
in front of screens, busy with buy and sell.
Lady Nature's material duty
helped create an artificial beauty
that lured the disobedient to choose
creations guided by a godly ruse:
artistic endeavors of love, with hope
communing goes beyond a queen or pope.
'Twas not democracy or ruled by king,
and hymns Karl composed for spirits to sing
were but a wispy thread of the voices
that thought free will accepted bad choices,
'til karma wrought the community's need
to craft a scapegoat for a new fruit's seed:
forbidden by Pharisees as fiction,
laws of love renewed by crucifixion.
Karl wanted to rig a personal self
that freed him to not be books on a shelf,
or a pawn in the light, lost in intrigues
as faiths divided then rejoined in leagues

to control and steer resources of Earth,
sapping energy because a high-berth
was granted them by a manifest right,
either through god or the power to smite.
Karl thought: Should I give the devil his due?
They are watching me to see what I do.
Then they block me out and spawn their mimics,
trying to control a composite mix
of rigged compulsions for economies
praised as wish-fulfillers, and enemies
are crafted to direct anger towards,
who also believe they have righteous swords.
Identifying with them, I would lose
a true base of power through those who choose
me as a guide to the new law movement,
free from the will of micro-management
instilled by the high-tech corporations
staging Armageddon among nations
so they can control the ensuing peace
with the Adam and Eve's gratitude lease
in an undisturbed bliss of consuming,
with only one law placed in their grooming.
They would not know love or how to create,
but do I want imitators whose fate
I am responsible for when all Hell
is harrowed because I choose to rebel?
Karl felt the closing of his escape-routes:
drank too long too often so bottle bouts
funneled him for release in fermented
grains and fruits as carefree and demented.
It seemed an easier path, but also
a traditional means for seeds to sow.
Numbers and shades could likewise be a way
to steer a resurrection's dawning ray,
which had no pain, or him as sacrifice
as manipulator of artifice.

He had summoned powers and his maze-web
had ensnared him with light that did not ebb.
Where he went, 'twas before him, and behind:
beyond the personal grid he designed.
His desire had been to be thought first-rate
in guiding ghosts and corporeal state.
Now that he felt he linked to others' fear
of the light, he hid in his cavern's rear,
which had some darkness in which to abide;
yet the light understood where he would hide,
and humored Karl's homosexual side,
but kept a bliss that did not want to know
the acts of vanity groomed for that show.
Karl thought the whites could have one of their breed
rise up and rule, though doomed not to succeed
against the global conglomerate state,
just as had Julian the Apostate
sought to revive the ancient traditions,
evolved to be corporate perditions,
which punished those deemed of insincere faith
by Ricky Rodent's world-media wraith.
One-dimensional living is a mere
step from being pushed in voids by a gear.
Ricky Rodent tarot cards could be gamed,
as could his casinos, with others blamed.
At Luell's place, Gravesend felt a hard pierce
sear through his soul's frame, which made him more fierce.
They had milled about after Squirrel-girl
reported their boss retired from the swirl,
which swept in turmoil through galactic space,
leaving fiends alone in their Yote hunt-chase.
Squirrel-girl had left for her own actions,
while Gravesend pondered what sundry factions
would pursue after unleashed on their own,
working at cross-purposes with seeds sown
among their favorites, and then hinder

opponents to be burnt to a cinder.
Views of open paths looked smoky and dense,
and some fiends even spoke of repentance.
Gravesend did not want such a drastic change,
not while there was a chance to rearrange
control and scattering through human plots
to seek a perfect state that quickly rots.
Putin's covert acts made him paranoid
of revenge-hunts putting him in the Void.
A career of wrecking people scared him
through fantasies which were cruel and dim;
spiteful fear would rather have World War Three's
staging than face reactions for decrees.
He found out that being a covert liege
differs from leading an armed forces' siege.
Putin was sugar-daddy to Trump's whores,
and wanted Yanks to avoid Ukraine's wars,
which was slowly being controlled by troops
Russia sent in to test new army groups:
an untried generation with new toys,
while Trump rallies Congress' cronies with noise,
lashing them on to again stand as chief
of government by a tyrant's belief.
Gravesend decided to let the new Yote
go free because he followed no trail's rote,
and might be useful in free will's battle,
when new shepherds rose for human cattle.
The realized Vishnu would create links
that would enslave fiends unless they found chinks
to hammer through Vishnu and his order
so Gravesend and fiends ranged without border.
Karl was no problem. Why make a big fuss
of Thunderbirds shaping an Icarus
who thought he would never be an angel
who falls when righteous Heaven makes a cull?
Fleeing in his duty of webs and maze,

Karl thought to be a prince of the next phase.
His weird communion was less of a threat
than the weapons' knowledge of Vishnu's het.
Though the *Christos'* light had long histories
of Earthly armed forces and their decrees,
Gravesend was on another plane of war
soul-steering, as was Vishnu's chore.
The spirit's strength was a greater trial
than high-tech weapons duped by hacker-guile.
It was better to demoralize souls
than waging war of huge body-count tolls,
because victors would always build anew,
but corrupt seeds could be fun in Vishnu.
Besides, the challenge of a spirit's fare
rose above tinkering with the hardware
weapons that had their own kind of devils,
who developed unique slaughter-revels;
interference in their territory
could be much resented and turn gory.
The fiends returned from tracking Vishnu's ghost
in an astral drift, near its human host,
which was weakened by a fast and blood loss,
ripe for the fiends to turn to pudding sauce.
The squad encouraged Gravesend of the thrill
that though Yote escaped, breaking Vishnu's will
would open more channels for them to roam,
and trick meditators on quarter's aum.
While their hopes were high, Gravesend reflected
they could either herd the souls selected,
and train them in the fiends' drill instruction,
or battle Vishnu now to destruction.
Gravesend's troops were few, though combat-hardy,
and Vishnu might have his own war-party.
Yet if victory was wrought, 'twould be great,
and other good shepherds might abdicate.
Lost souls the fiends garnered were less worthwhile

than restructuring faiths to the fiends' style.
Gravesend looked at Ned, passed out on the floor,
and Gravesend chose the task to test his lore.
Open astral-space of Samsara's sea
would be traveled to with fierce urgency.
Gravesend declared this to the devils' cheer:
no longer trapped with a fool drunk on beer
and crazed from an opioid consumption,
nearing the throes of a bad conniption.
They prepared their charms, did a weapons' check,
then left Ned Luell in his wastrel dreck.
Numbers encompassed Vishnu's changing mind,
each proclaimed it had Ideals designed
for enlightenment that brought a treasure
beyond the clay that time and space measure.
When he was tempted, the numbers folded
to labyrinths, which if entered, molded
Vishnu's glazed mind to an infinite chase
that promised connections through all of space.
His body was in a sleep-deprived state,
yet knew using the first principle trait
would bring his drifting realized spirit
to Earth by means of what the Hindu's writ:
waking, dreaming, dreamless state, and beyond,
were the quarters of aum's Samsara pond.
So Vishnu focused on the number four,
clearing each stage of karma to true lore.
Thus he tried to direct his astral shape
with one Ideal number for escape.
Aum starts, a middle, the end, and beyond,
with him as the sustainer of what dawned.
Dan Tines' shag-herb had no place in the rite
of new Vishnu curbing his appetite,
instead let visions and space return him,
having gathered Hindu zones and its hymn.
Gurus, medicine men and women saw

him reaching Earth's bubble, defying law.
The tunnels through Earth's atmosphere were shocked
by a laughter that had Gravity mocked,
who thought at first his Lady had gone wild,
and he prepared to smite what she had styled;
then he saw Gravesend's fiends clear the tunnels
like tornados ripping with cloud funnels.
The laughter chilled Gravity by its tone
of fighting Zen masters freed from a koan.
Riddles had never amused Gravity:
his job was matter, and integrity
kept silly questions in vast, stupid mists
like inquiries by astrophysicists.
Gravity did his job, and solutions
were always changed by his revolutions.
Taking different roles for new rewards
tethered stars and people to warping cords.
They had voted and won democracy;
yet, like Dan Tines, still loved a fantasy
that seemed open-ended, with a trophy
for songs beyond a corporate strophe.
Images blur from one phase to the next,
as seasons change to have consumers hexed
by subliminal codes that go soul-deep
of sport-faces to herd screen-crowds like sheep,
with holidays to rev economies
centered on entertainment industries.
Escape-routes shuddered through the corralled souls,
as Vishnu was a threat near funnel-holes,
upsetting status systems and the guides
of proxy-livers through fantasy tides
rolling and competing through the airwaves,
herding to teach how a good soul behaves.
The gurus had watched as Vishnu returned,
some were firm believers, but a few spurned
any renovations in their belief

which Vishnu compelled to their loss and grief.
Dan Tines knew escape-routes were important;
booze had been his, with many doomed portent,
which he often laughed off as destiny
for Bacchus/Christ communing agony.
Dan Tines wondered how Vishnu would portray
himself as guide or a soul gone astray.
For he had been drifting through astral space,
perhaps collecting versions of his face
so his images could be many things
to different people so each one sings
an individual faith that collects
to be one hymn to god through all the sects.
Trailing Vishnu were scribes Ganesha sped
to record the advent-fight being bred.
God, soul, reason, and nature were combined
to fight for directions of a new mind.
'Tis easy for synthetic escape-routes
to be waylaid towards corporate bouts.
Some schemed for versions of propaganda
to sell in a corporate agenda
for proxy-livers to experience,
though some joined the fight for a pure essence.
A guru waited with his acolytes
at the top of a tunnel, near the lights
that preceded Vishnu's returning form.
Gravesend emerged with his squad like a storm
blazing against the guru and his troops,
who tried to catch the fiends in astral loops.
In desperate fury, fiends cut their way
from snares, and to the acolytes' dismay,
the fiends aimed at the meditating liege
who sat in the eye of the typhoon siege,
directing his team by his inner orb
on lotus plants, whose strength he could absorb.
Dirty-toe reached the guru and slashed hard

with a spear, and cries from the guru's bard
rang like a blessing among Gravesend's squad,
as their foes burst like a cottonwood pod,
and blew away in many directions.
Dirty-toe licked his spear like confections
of sugary taste ran along its point,
and the guru knew his strength would anoint
Dirty-toe to high-levels of insight
that would be ordered to use against right
structure and the need for stability,
which Vishnu performed as his main duty.
The guru thought he was a manifest
part of Vishnu, and had fought to be blest
within the holy regions of the lord,
but Dirty-toe owned that piece, and his horde
might conquer other bits of Vishnu's realm,
and turn loose the rapture of free will's helm.
Skirmishes broke out before battle-lines
were ordered and drawn to fighting designs.
Gurus and swamis split into factions
for glories of influencing actions
by Lord Vishnu, who could render control
over others to a special, blessed soul.
Guru Prabi encircled Happy-trash
with rings of lightning swords that hummed a clash.
The fiend, believing it an illusion,
raced at them and was chopped to diffusion
that spread his astral spirit to a wreck,
which would take centuries to reconnect.
Proud of his conquest, Guru Prabi turned
to another fiend whose soul should be burned,
but Law-breaker saw how his comrade fell,
and redirected Guru Prabi's spell
so it spread the swords through his acolytes,
cleaving them to motes of shrieking, crushed lights.
Law-breaker grabbed the last lightning saber,

his adrenalin high from the labor,
and rushed to slay the guru, who stayed set
and immobile as he summoned a het,
who should have protected their teacher-guide,
but their courage deflated when applied
to the raging fiend on a berserk spree,
so they did not heed their master's decree,
but watched Law-breaker flash the lightning sword,
and like a mad bull had the guru gored.
Searing curses howled from his destroyed ghost,
so blights crushed those whom he led as a host.
Rashti, a prince of the warrior-caste,
saw the future would be a shattered past
if the believers did not formulate
a strategy that had the fiends deflate
from their glorious pell-mell rampaging,
rather than forced to a plotted staging
of battle-lines drawn in Hindu tactics,
as gurus worked their mantras and bead-ticks.
Rashti ordered the faithful to withdraw,
leaving some behind, as if in a maw
of gnashing fangs that glittered hate and blood,
trapped by the fiends to be chewed on like cud.
The chief-guru resented Rashti's plan,
which seemed to usurp the chief's governed clan;
warriors should not replace a guru,
and put him to shame in front of a crew.
While they argued near Vishnu's astral shape,
the fiends circled those who did not escape.
Splat-nose seized a dead soldier's spear and shield,
and led a charge in the surrounded field
to where a young warrior bravely fought
for the soul of a swami who was caught
among fiends, like the head of a viper,
which has become aggressive and hyper.
The swami sang a death-chant for his soul

to guide it from taking another role,
to a peace beyond all understanding,
while Splat-nose tightened the fiends' loose banding,
until the Hindus had no place to move,
but the young guard still had courage to prove
that he was no weakling, and slashed a strike,
which cut off the left arm of Hairy-spike.
He shuddered and howled at the piercing pain,
and his soul fell from the war's astral-plane.
Honey-spot quickly filled the empty place,
plotting revenge for Hairy-spike's disgrace.
He had been her friend and sometime lover,
and thick dark energy seemed to hover
about Honey-spot's charm and wicked blade,
wanting to prove her worth in vengeance-trade.
She put on a display of her prowess,
forcing the warrior back in distress,
whose swami counted beads while voicing chants,
trying to out-pray the fiends' shrieking rants.
The Hindu warrior threw a sly knife
that slit Honey-spot's throat, ending her strife.
Her fellows screamed with rage and did not wait
to concert an attack to vent their hate.
They fell on the soldier and his teacher,
shredding them to ruin every feature.
Rashti told the guru: "Cross-purposes
are failing; we must unite our poses
to a single fighting plan we contrive
if we wish to live and Vishnu survive.
He wounded himself on Earth and suffers
from fiends' ghastly pains, which we as buffers
have failed to protect our great lord against,
and their hope grows while we become incensed
with each other, having no single course,
all of us fighting to be the white horse
that the last avatar of Vishnu rides

in the upheaval of Samsara's tides."
The guru smiled: "It is your soldier's lot
to form ranks and free our lord for the plot
of the story to have a grand finish;
thus, I will give orders to relinquish
my troops to you, and use diplomacy
with my colleagues so that you oversee
all the soldiers, while we gather to pray
Vishnu to his body, and not be prey."
Guru Hil noticed the stars were blinking
fight codes to troops, and he began thinking:
I have heard that some white teachers of tales
are paid to warp stories to mainstream rales
that destroy their white male competition,
teaching them they should have no fruition
because they would be evil patriarchs,
who would have upon them the devil's marks,
so leave baby-making to better men,
and if they go bad, blame white males again.
Thus eugenics, taught as literature,
caught up with whites and threatens their future.
Diversifieds vilify eugenics
then buy perfect baby gene-mechanics.
Putting story-lines in professors' keep
is like a celibate priest teaching sheep
that contraceptives are the devils' tools,
then nuts competing rams to guide gene-pools.
So the monopoly of stories buy
filial duty to management by
a non-specific gender corporate
parent whose subsidiaries owe credit.
To control those in the third-dimension,
make screen-selves of them lack dissension,
while rewiring their electric brain-cells
to prefer obedience than dank Hells.
A lightning flash from a lady or lord

on a screen that zaps through the spinal cord
gathers believers in celebrities,
like thunderstorms of now dead deities.
Folks forget each other in servitude
to the *deus ex machine* attitude,
which seeks to control duties of my liege
through their service to him in this wild siege.
They are like stars who each have a station
in outlined plans of a constellation;
just as we each want a piece of Vishnu
to influence a system we renew.

16

Filling Hieroglyphs

To Yote the world appeared empty and bleak;
as if Earth itself had sprung a bad leak,
and all the resources were drained to build
images that could never be fulfilled.
What did it matter Yote felt left behind?
He was not of hollow humans designed
to lead an insurrection or commune
to others they should constantly consume.
Smog from the fires was like smoky entrails
sent to Elder gods as sacrifice grails.
Hollywood Babylon offered its dregs
to keep Yote reeling and off of his legs.
He heard Vishnu's Aum, and Yote's hackles raised:
the old and the new stars would have him phased
into oblivion as they battled
for societies that shook and rattled.
He saw himself well-trained, led by a leash,
and snarled with rage at the vision-pastiche.
Vishnu's potency aimed down the tunnels
and were met with cloudy colored funnels,
which were separated as directions,
though the last one, red, refused connections.
Yote watched with glee as red fought to maintain
its own spiritual essence and pain.

It refused to serve a hierarchy
that sold addiction for security.
Though it was new, the old songs had been passed
for its keeping, not to support a caste.
So what if space and time's stability
offered new directions ability?
Yote felt a wholeness watching that Quarter
refuse to serve square hives of brick-mortar.
Red danced away, then lingered in eye-spots,
as Vishnu's host tried to collect its dots.
Gurus and part of Vishnu's consciousness
formed about Coyote with an address:
"We are shaping a direction for souls
that are defined beyond corporate roles,
and the fight can be won through connections
to the rising Four Quarters' directions.
If the demons defeat us, then the task
of story-lives will be the song and mask
of corporations that deal with demons
to stage screen scripts of self-fulfilled omens.
We prefer a smooth continuous route,
where gory mayhem does not splash and spout
just to support our beliefs and free will,
but if 'tis the end, we reap what we till.
You understand the North Direction well,
because you also pose as a rebel;
but you must understand that your story
is nothing compared to Vishnu's glory,
and the ensuing peace that can prevail
when the *Christos* achieves its Holy Grail,
which will replace corporate water-muck,
and not force spirits to finally shuck
bodies due to raiding human-made germs
that inherit the world as false-tongued worms.
Recruit the North and you will find beauty
beyond horrors of corporate duty.

Our structure is built for long endurance,
and all of your tricks and skills shall enhance,
for you are noble and worthy of hire,
beyond the tuning of an arranged choir.
You are free to wander the blighted land,
and by subtle means can win North as planned.
Your reward will be a territory,
and a place in our epic history.
Receive a bit of essence of Vishnu,
that we pass through the tunnels unto you."
Healing calm washed away the entropy
of the beast that chased Yote with its strophe.
A soothing release flittered through his skull
from links to Vishnu's buddhi-tentacle.
The gurus' flattery had warmed Yote's heart,
as did promised rewards to play his part.
He was not humble but ignored voices
that said Vishnu was the best of choices.
Yote began to pad with untiring feet
to the North, ready to dare any feat.
The areas he passed began to bloom
with shining dew and flowers like a loom
woven through the fabric of the desert,
as Lady Nature began to assert
her inherited powers, and hovered
about Coyote, keeping him covered
in a shadowy mist, hidden from sight,
as the lands he passed through reached a new height
of unspoiled colors and life of brilliance,
and the smog parted with her salience,
following Yote on his long trek to find
the last Direction in the Quarters' bind.
Yet she also had her own schemes to ploy,
and Yote would be sufficient to employ.
She slowly slipped bits of Vishnu's essence
into creatures Yote passed, filling each sense.

A lizard gazed at the glorious sight,
then a road-runner snatched him with one bite.
A mouse thought what to give rather than take,
and was promptly swallowed whole by a snake.
So life went behind Yote blazing his trails:
light finding ways to predators' entrails.
Officials do not get bribes from the poor
of their nations to relieve hunger's core.
Lady Nature would have the best for plots
formed from where spirits placed their astral spots.
Clans and tribes would rise to bestow their thanks,
and karma would go beyond credit banks.
Once again, the old songs would inspire dance:
reason beyond synthetic ignorance
to learn again animal nations' tongues,
and respect the food-chain's many-tiered rungs.
A king is worm-bait; the dust of peons'
rises forever throughout the eons.
Men manipulated for beatitudes,
which synthesized women's true attitudes,
who learn to play the false game of image
as a saving grace posing as knowledge.
Like Egyptian gods consumed their faithful
to purify them, and their waste made null,
and as enlightened energy they moved
through the worlds beyond what Gravity grooved;
so Nature reformed from bottom to top,
her little face in consumer and crop.
She spread her hope's light as the temptations
began to weave from civilized nations.
She separated the rows, skilled and deft:
women go to the right, males to the left.
She walked the gauntlet as they neared frenzy,
stirred in a roiling dance of ecstasy.
When she neared the apex, the rows collapsed;
she seethed rage, and after a moment lapsed,

images appeared of a new control,
offering her peace and a leading role.
Lightning cogs and wheels of fortune that spun
for thinning the herds or simply for fun.
Easier ways to play men off of men
to get the Alpha for her own amen.
Quicker means to revenge and dole rewards,
with cheating allowed by ladies and lords,
so long as she graciously gave tribute
to them, and did not eat knowledge's fruit.
Substance and reason were to be guided
in all the desires where she abided.
New Lady Nature saw the former Miss
laying in bed in a drunk black-out bliss.
Nature peeled some webs from the writhing form,
who flashed a solitary lightning-storm.
A shriek pealed out along with the large thread,
which wove round the world with voices who said:
"Keep sending messengers we can nail-up
for new covenants and communion-cup,
and will reform them to our images
when machines run low on fuming mages,
and all the stars split to their own orbits
to run the show you record without wits.
Rama Ron's celebrity stars' fixture
survived Charles Manson's rebellious mixture,
but now everyone has a performance,
and a camera to record their chance
at being part of new constellations
as oracles for media stations.
We watch you use a subtle agency
to build a god or a blest regency
greedy for gold or the elephants' tusks,
draining humanity to leave our husks.
Whether Arabia or Israel,
you rig a response like Pavlov's dog-bell.

Your own people go hungry, while you send
funds to foreign lands, with kickbacks to blend
your armies to their dirty, nasty wars,
then sell them the rewards like corrupt whores.
The artificial selections' awards
are underground snakes that noose finance-cords.
We may yet be able to change the course
of war-oracles in the *Bible*'s source
and cyber-kinetic polluted haze
that promises a wish-fulfilling phase."
The web slowly ran to a silent gloom,
and she wondered if it fit on her loom,
or give it back to old Lady Nature
as an inherent part of her feature.
They both needed protection from the scenes
which evolved temptation through Soma weans
unto the next levels of consumption
that left some behind, with bad exemption
if they failed to invest in the dramas
which promised life without any traumas.
What did the two of them have to offer
except a body as a soul's coffer?
The new Lady sat in a thoughtful trance,
as the former leapt at the risky chance,
and poured her potency into the wild,
spiting the rest for being tame and mild.
The new Lady watched this, and bit her lip,
as balance turmoiled and began to slip.
She thought: They will bring Hell upon their own;
civilized states cannot stand wild seeds sown.
An order of pageantry has evolved
that pretends to have our wild nature solved
through temptations of imagery that hold
reflections of us we think should be sold
as part of the globe's program enterprise,
yet only win a one-dimension prize,

and use it to buy our protected lairs,
where we practice our shows to win more wares.
Where would she have the best story to tell
of the three divisions: Heaven, Sea, Hell?
Satellite space offered the shades' networks,
collected to display one's power quirks;
which Hell reflected without much content:
snaking cords for money-messages sent.
She chose Samsara, life's deathly ocean,
to mix bodies' water with a potion.
Predators could be quelled for times of peace
and protect lands where she had her own lease.
Plants and animal parts provided charms,
but not manage it like corporate farms.
They could be held on tight reins, meek and mild,
and yet grant them periods to be wild.
As if to purposely upset her plans,
white conglomerates displayed their own clans.
The fury of brains after a hard wash
was like something from Hieronymus Bosh.
Outnumbering foes, five-hundred to one,
tough-guys pillaged like Attila the Hun,
or *A Clockwork Orange*: droog dissidents
near beat-up an old lady and lynched Pence
when screen-guides led by Trump stirred an assault,
but Republicans said 'twas not Trump's fault
at impeachment hearings to strip the pledge
that taxpayers owe Trump his privilege:
while they go sick and hungry, his greed-head
is pensioned by taxes to be well-fed.
Screen guilds realized their foundering ship
was hijacked unless they used censorship.
Fear ran rampant in the guarded nation,
which furthered its militarization.
Yote kept on his feet during the weird blast,
hunting for a means of life that would last.

The Hindus could structure their own caste-state,
and many lands might want to imitate
China's corporate military style;
even Russia swelled in an angry rile,
which could mean Putin was nearly played-out,
so the hatchet-men spoiling for a bout
were replaced with soft hands in iron-gloves,
and folks attached to screen-ideal loves.
Protected Edens might grant open space
for Yote to practice his shape-shifting face.
Oral stories of his ranging exploits
were more suited to him than what anoints
leaders to believe their holy missions
need obedience to their decisions.
Yote would help corralling the Quarter flocks,
then slip free and go where there were no locks.
He was a wily trickster once again,
who snared them in a repeating omen.
Heaven was not lowered to his standards,
but he would aid them, collecting their shards
to reform them and renovate a guide,
and Lady Nature helped increase his stride.
Yote was used to horror that had a point
in forming people to want to anoint
someone for stability and trading.
The pointless horrors of old stars fading,
and their spiteful destruction so new stars
would only inherit polluted mars,
were terrors that made wasteland voices shriek
'twas time old deities of fire to wreak
havoc until only ashes remain,
and the Void once again had sole domain.
All would die equally and be unfit
to punish Armageddon's staged profit.
Memories of synthetic paradise
could be rewarded to some, with a price.

Such shapeless forms haunted Yote's every step,
howling he threatened their vigor and pep,
leaving them in the Void, struck by belief
that promised an end to their Earthly grief.
To Yote, the horror seemed pointless and vain:
wanting immortality with no stain,
which left them in the Void of guilty faiths
trampling Earth to locate Paraclete wraiths.
The parting tides that welcomed Yote's travel
turned dark as the spirits tried to ravel
their wispy souls to what was promised them
if they invested in the right system.
Their spirits were woven fates to the scenes
mass-manufactured by the gods' machines.
Desert sands turned to icy sheets of snow,
as spirits revolved bleakly, row on row.
Some killed for pleasure, were haunted by ghosts,
and cast out from the communion of hosts.
They put the fear of god into humans
for enjoyment, now were severed from clans
whose systems had their own deities' wrath
that focused on rewards for a true path.
A rising tundra followed the flat grange,
then Yote was passing through a mountain range.
He heard the lost wailing which blamed the gods
who had granted the might to crush with rods,
and now the gods claimed it was a bad job
for being the rage instilled in the mob.
A ghost separated to pace with Yote:
it burned with vengeance, yet a tiny mote.
Its eyes gleamed wildly as it struggled from
the spinning spirits and their shrilling hum.
Yote kept walking from the pointless horror,
as the ghost tried to speak above the roar:
"Loyalty based on standard of living
shocks businesses who control divvying.

We gave Ukraine money and corruption,
then threatened the funds with a disruption
if they did not clean out the rot we bought;
so sold themselves to Russia, and are caught
in a civil war, which is a proxy
struggle of bribes and weapons gone crazy.
When life-styles are threatened, selling one's soul
to rebel against the lead master-role
makes what were proxy-fights turn personal
because they refuse to be collected
for shepherding culls by the selected.
Franchising governments makes a schism,
yet they expect great patriotism
and personal fealties, which might meet
an opposing mutiny out in the street.
If they are only hollow shades on screens,
then I owe myself to make better scenes.
Trump in-person would not lead as crowds charged,
for he lacks dimension, though screen-enlarged,
just like his chumps, who outnumbered the guards,
heeding wails of oracle cyber-bards.
When the troops arrived at the Capitol,
gangs passively left in a sullen stroll."
Yote sped from the apostate hard-lucker;
like Trump said, why throw in with a sucker?
While he was atop the gold ladder's gang,
they were snared in the dirty tricks he sprang.
The whirling swept the soul back to its grind,
and Yote left the aimless horrors behind,
not caring which direction was its goal,
or if its fragments washed-up on a shoal.
The monopolies on people and wares
brought Ted Roosevelt, with investment fares
hollering; 'We bought the son of a bitch,
but he did not stay bought.' Which caused a glitch.
The howls followed Yote from the mountain's peak,

wanting a prophet to guide their mystique.
Demanding someone incarnate a Cause
to rise them above micro-managed laws
to be at the top of the cogs and wheels,
and dominate *deus ex machina* deals.
Why they believed that Trump, a screen-made man,
embodied a violent Cause, which ran
risks of danger he is known to avoid,
must be due to his fans own paranoid
stirrings through too much screen-time dimensions,
which shook already weak comprehensions,
and their notions of true reality
were bats in belfries gone mad and flitty.
Falsehoods are evil on computer-sites,
but stealing others' work does not bring smites
if duly employed by Rick Rodent's squads
absorbing media foes for seed-pods
that game influence with illusive lies,
which they accuse others of with loud cries.
Their missionary work-plans spread their sect,
like Jesuits, after Iran is wrecked.
The world ends hollowly, without a core,
whimpering at a self-image horror.
To sustain artificial existence,
the rigged cords of Fate become strained and tense,
and the price Earth pays is no shallow cost:
the third-dimension is the holocaust
sacrifice to achieve programmed pleasures,
with saviors to dole out scripted treasures.
Their hollow wraith's wish for a fiery flood
was ignored by Yote, who was after blood.
His eyes were red, like the sun on stained glass,
yet beyond Heaven's Hound hunting church-Mass.
He went down a cleft and followed the spurs
of the mountains, which became snow-capped blurs,
replaced by rows of hills that jut branches,

isolating towns and cattle ranches.
His goal was near and he shook melted snow
off his pelt as if in a wriggly throe.
His senses were heightened by Vishnu's pact,
and he loped through curves of the last hills' tract.
He slowed to eat mice, feeling ravenous,
and was not drawn into self-consciousness
by his five senses that had connections
to mass-buddhi wanting Yote's selections
of free will to follow all their choices
to add his song to their sundry voices.
Perhaps they were astral spots in the stars,
gathering energy with psychic spars
for fights against opposites to take roles
which had rewards that rose them above proles
with breeding and multiplying sex ads,
which pursued or invented trendy fads.
Each sense carried thoughts to a group that chose
how the particular thought made its pose
in Yote's mind, blending as an image force
of pleasure or pain for their chosen course;
controlling Yote as a guiding factor
through all his shape-shifting as an actor.
Yote detached, yet still sifted through the forms,
which were revealed at first like lightning-storms.
When they knew he could not be scared or lured
to attach to offered shapes as if cured
of mortality by ruling them all,
they slowed the image-making to enthrall
with temptations of females and a verse
they sang and danced to for Yote to immerse.
Yote's canny mind knew how they used reason,
but females are not temptations' treason
committed by Coyote on himself,
and were more fun than books on Dan Tines' shelf,
who was in a small region of Yote's brain,

using ancient lore as a pathway lane
to link the past with trails of the future,
patching some traditions with a suture.
Tines knew how 'twas to judge horrors and hurts,
having once styled himself as Shiva Kurtz,
a white criminal-deity whose means
were a method of madness through all the scenes
Ganesha had wrote as a whirling maze,
'til with his tusks was forced to the next phase.
At first, Yote thought it as a white man's trick,
who tried to spread light with a switch's flick,
and the machine of the gods would trap Yote
to domesticate him or skin his coat.
Yet Tines let Coyote run the mind-halls,
avoiding the Sirens' reef-crashing calls.
Then Yote slowed down in a room of mirrors,
and chose one, thinking: I want to be hers.
She was a wizened woman, whose wrinkles
shifted like quakes when she smiled creased crinkles.
Yote had stopped at a less-traveled highway
during his mind's journey for roles to play.
He trusted god's fate, not the command-chain,
so rewards were his own, as was the pain.
He heard a truck's engine nearing his post,
and shaped to the old lady as her host.
In the cab of the truck, Ben Eagle Claw's
mind was beyond hypocritical laws.
He would enforce rule, for a big ration,
on his blighted Native reservation,
who needed money and a ruling clan.
With his distant cousin, Joby, their plan
would earn booty to stabilize orders,
and steal casino-wealth from the hoarders.
The other three dominant families
would be forced under to say homilies
for their dead, which would most likely occur

when his clan made moves with flying of fur.
Their voyage was to gain outsider aid:
females for weapons of a higher-grade
than two-barreled shotguns or a rifle
that scares a moment but does not stifle
a return attack of deadly intent,
perhaps in an ambush where lives are spent.
The drug-trade would likely be up for grabs,
needing an enforcer for credit-tabs;
it was a business that fit Joby's style,
as he was greedy and easy to rile.
The women would also buy-off police,
and the Mafia boss would rent the lease
of the casino's machines to Ben's side,
trading the women as whores for a ride.
Ben drove as the females in the trailer
reeled in filth, waiting for their next jailer.
As he drove, Ben stayed focused on the road,
trying not to think of a moral code
beyond the ties to a family-sect,
rather than hopes and prayers that genuflect
on corporations as wish-fulfillers,
reputed as society's pillars.
He crested a slope and saw a being
beside the road, her voice a sharp keening
of agonized lament, dressed in tatters.
It was Coyote who changed his matters
to the woman in his psychic-mirrors,
which was not a pointless den of horrors.
Ben swerved a bit and checked the reflections
of the truck's looking-glass, but refractions
of instant light blinded him so he blinked,
wondering if he and after-lives linked.
He could not get the image from his head,
so he shook Joby awake and Ben said:
"I think maybe you should drive for a while.

I just saw a hitch-hiker in the style
and full appearance of my grandmother,
so you drive before she makes another
display that depresses me on this job,
accusing me with a soul-rending sob
that I betray the blood of our own tribe
and heritage for the means to out-bribe
our foes also misled by outsiders
as to who will be the savior riders
on the horses of the apocalypse
the prophets foretold, hot coal put to lips.
We have bought into their chicanery
because we like convenient finery,
so when they act their Armageddon script,
their fires of doom will also have us stripped.
She made my outfit as I learned to dance,
and taught me not to play rigged games of chance.
She has been dead seven years, and she wore
the last fancy-dress she made with her lore,
though 'twas in rags and her bearing seemed lost.
It made me wonder of our incurred cost.
'Tis not like we sell blood for beer-money,
or pet shops that sell an Easter bunny.
Our own tribal consciousness is retail,
like looting Crusaders after the Grail."
Joby sneered: "We do not play at fiction,
so work on no romantic depiction.
Money-changing has evolved through the years,
but we still have to round herds for the shears.
Even if money is artificial,
it buys protection that is official.
Money that buys stories changes the state,
guiding versions to feast or famine fate.
When land and water give out through Death's carve,
and only the rich do not grub and starve,
like entertainers and politicians,

perhaps rebellions will have fruitions;
until then, why be hungry or upset
at the dangling hooked bait we never get?
African homies sold wives as livestock,
as if they were goats or a chicken-flock.
Women were traded in our ancient days,
so what makes you think humans changed their ways,
except for the market going high-tech,
and money being a tiny byte-speck?
Channeled like some Mayan ghost-god of wealth,
so the rich can slowly withdraw in stealth,
and leave the rest of us in barren fields.
They have castles that Ricky Rodent shields,
and ziggurats like Babylon god-kings,
who rule according to dreams' calm or stings.
Do you desire to be at the mercy
of Caligula at war with the sea,
or visions of global democracy?
We got rid of Trump starring as Otho
in a Roman government overthrow.
Money buys more than just being alive.
I did my eight hours, 'tis your turn to drive,
and give it a rest about the drama
of seeing the spirit of your grandma."
What one does on the streets, which others shun,
can gain a fine living and a mansion;
like Fielding's Jonathon Wilde to Walpole,
extreme criminal types run pole-to-pole.
If big games are rigged, then betting reports
carry more influence than legal courts,
and Joby's reservation could make cash
on sports through the puppet-master's news flash;
such information was valuable
and rare to keep the odds' market stable,
so suspicions were steered from secret crimes
'til the betters were drained of their last dimes.

Joby's circus emperor's thumb turned down
on being a poor, drunk performing clown.
As money quickly changed its qualities,
people bought in for shares of quantities.
One could gamble from anywhere using
computers for a festive carousing.
The new coliseum is a home-show,
and winning broadcasts usurped the stars' glow,
rendering unto synthetic faces
that created new routes through air-spaces.
Artificial money has no image
declaring a nation's solemn pay-pledge.
Render unto a face what is its own,
and be Caesar spreading yours as a loan.
Rome's subculture had years of practiced craft,
but Natives learned quick about bribes and graft.
The main problem was a lack of blood-links
the mob used as *omerta* fear-techniques,
and better funds to buy an official,
so when Natives bought in, the initial
rewards seemed worth the price of admission,
'til betrayed by the mob's competition.
Joby's clan was willing to take chances,
so he did not want to hear of dances
that Ben and his grandma did long ago,
when he should focus driving the cargo.
Their clan leader would despise some mind-trick
that abruptly turned Ben a romantic.
They spent three days staying sober and clean
to prepare for the trip and buy a lien
which would make them the most powerful clan,
and like Jews on their foes, whip up a Ban
on families of the reservation
who had their own plans of wealth's salvation.
Ben vacillated in his loyalty;
his clan wanted to be like royalty,

and if they were not loved, they would be feared,
but when the ghost of his grandma appeared,
Ben suffered a fright he could not by-pass,
and he saw the gathering of a mass,
in the dusk, of crimson clouds spun in flight,
and Thunderbirds descended from their height.
They passed over, dancing with whirls and spins,
and Ben cringed in his seat, accused of sins.
He had been a dancer above the sea
of life's deathly ocean, in ecstasy;
and the animal nations joined the host
without the violence and bragging boast
inherent in diverse underworld crime,
that some set to machine-music and rhyme.
Ben's grandma reappeared, more than a blur,
then Yote raced ahead for the ocular
ghost to haunt Ben to a paranoid mote,
adrift with the Thunderbirds' singing note.
Coyote summoned Raven for Ben's soul
to be washed on the Thunderbirds' atoll.
They had made a circle like coral reefs,
and the center was an island of griefs.
Ben saw Raven flying toward the truck,
and knew the bird would make Ben's body shuck
his spirit, which was unacceptable,
for he brought no thing good to the table
in after-life's feast of principle joy,
except cruel tendencies to destroy.
Ben thought: Now is not the time to panic,
though 'tis more than a moment of manic
frenzy that the spirits forming designs
will steal my soul if I ignore their signs.
'Tis beyond my reason or will power
that my destiny is shaped to this hour.
He slowed the truck and steered to the roadside,
as the gavotting spirits swarmed a tide.

Jolted awake, Joby screamed in fury
they could not goof-off, were in a hurry.
Ben parked, took the keys from the ignition,
and said it was the end of their mission.
He got out and walked to the carrier,
but standing in front as a barrier,
Joby pushed Ben back and swung a right fist
that would have broke Ben's jaw, but mostly missed.
Ben thought: Well now we have come down to it.
One seeing ghosts that induced a mad fit,
the other eager to be a gangster,
and we are finally caught in this stir.
How did I get the ambition to be
a pimp human-trafficking coyote?
Ben tucked in his chin and beveled his arms,
then jabbed a punch of ringing bell alarms
in Joby's brain, and his teeth cut his lip.
He stepped back, then swung a right, with his hip
rotating into the strike at Ben's nose,
which was partly blocked. They stood in a pose,
glaring at each other in defiance,
like a chemical lab of bad science
mixing contrary potions with no heed
of poison drafted from a wicked seed.
Joby had no gun because in a fit
of anger he would desire to use it;
the serious people they were to meet
might say something to turn-up Joby's heat,
and gunplay was not best diplomacy,
so the clan-chief disarmed that trip's posse.
Raven fluttered and perched on a fence-post,
watching the spirit who had Yote as host.
Both disliked using illusions to prove
life was an illusion that fit each groove.
The worlds had substance to be passed along,
so Raven was surprised the Hindus' song

had brought Yote to their faith of detachment
in fights of the Four Quarters' encroachment.
A stomach blow made Joby puke his lunch,
and Raven cawed the contest punch-by-punch.
Yote sat panting, as the woman he wore
tried to use his fatigue to steer his core.
Raven: "Brown-jacket has some broken ribs,
and is yakking like babies needing bibs.
Mohawk-head will not let him catch his wind,
acting as punisher on those who sinned.
This might be about a blessing or curse,
or just the profits from a prize-ring purse.
One always likes to have good and bad dudes
in battles so it heightens the fans' moods.
Brown-jacket kneed Mohawk-head in the thigh,
hoping attrition will slow the fist-fly.
Mohawk-head is taking more body-blows,
as Brown-jacket attempts to end the throes
in a flurry of punches that tire them,
so they clinch together like a seamed hem.
This is not a dance, so come on, fellows,
give us a fight and fan the war-bellows.
Mohawk-head just gave him a nasty cut
and broken nose from a wicked head-butt.
Brown-jacket is down, looks like for the count,
vaulting out of consciousness to dismount
on the gravel along the highway side,
his mind tumbling about a punch-drunk tide."
Ben stood panting, then unlocked the trailer,
yelling at the girls, who like a sailor,
had lost their land-legs, to pile out and run
to wherever they believed their fates spun.
A lass circled Joby, stomping his head;
when Ben asked what she was doing, she said:
"I am stamping out the evil he did,
and dancing circles to strangle his grid.

Join me and we will replenish our lives,
and send the bad spirits to hard nose-dives."
Ben paused, then Yote keened forth a dancing tune
that rose Ben's spirit to stamp out ruin.

17

Replacement Therapy

I n the Heavens the battle continued,
with decades of bad-blood purged in the feud.
The shades surrounded a young warrior
guarding his guru, when a spout foyer
erupted more shades from dark energy,
howling blasphemous chords of liturgy.
Gravesend watched, thinking: This is a duel
that promises all good and non-dual,
or a burst of creation with free will
addictions to patterns churned like a mill.
These astral shadows are unknown to me,
nor are they organized as an army.
My boss let go any control he had
in guarding his lot, now it has gone mad.
Underworld shades from distant galaxies
ride the currents of the tidal space seas.
Perhaps they return from a banishment,
not caring for rewards, but want to vent
a vengeance that destroys all in their path.
They pushed through my squad in a bloody swath,
and killed the Hindu guard and his guru,
whom I much respected for being true.
We had a difference on policies,
but needed one another's fallacies

to maintain cycles' contrary orders,
as corporations merge without borders,
selecting their spots of Edens to build,
which we invade with the knowledge we tilled
with the help of the holy, who aspire
to life beyond an ignorant empire.
Using some of Vishnu's strength to recruit
and drill new fiends from a different root
were the procedures both sides accepted,
just as there were fiends who left our fetid
existence and repented their story
for new roles in Heaven's territory.
The soul-blasting appetite on display
threatened all of Gravesend's fun with Earth's clay.
They mimicked the worst of all genera,
as if to devour the entire terra.
Gravesend lowered his head, filled with sour shame;
the unbalance caused was partly his blame.
On leaving his boss, Gravesend's free will failed,
and sat morosely, as a spirit sailed
from Earth to stand beside Gravesend and watch
the shadows turn souls to a crimson splotch.
Eager for sympathetic company
which would not drive Gravesend to a bent knee,
he said: "I am tired of being toyed with.
Perhaps I can find an evolving myth,
throwing myself in the Void to be doomed
so my knowledge of evil is consumed."
Part of Dan Tines' soul left his sleeping shape,
as the new communion replaced wine's grape.
Knowing his body was safely in bed,
Tines patted Gravesend's sunk shoulders and said:
"I did it, too, homeless without a shell
for protection against Heaven and Hell.
I followed webs through Iktomi's gulf
in volumes by Ganesh and Thomas Wolfe.

I was inspired to make bets I could hedge,
watching many snails crawl along the edge
of razors, and survive the pointless task
as a self-image caught behind a mask,
and wanting to buy more rewarding roles,
willing to invest in the highest tolls.
Credit is a gamble one can pay back
through a job that stays on the market's track,
so one has to mimic the command-chain,
and represent them without any stain.
I watched Tom Eliot and Joe Conrad
reformed to a diversified new fad,
and each version becomes a duller shade,
'til 'tis but a hollow voice being paid.
Some wealthy say, 'We should not grant the poor
a living-wage that spurs to ask for more,
because it makes them greedy and demand
enough to have an independent stand.
We save them from lifestyles of the greedy,
and we have their support, like a treaty.
By controlling access to our forums,
we keep them following our stale bread-crumbs.
We present them the stories that they buy,
believing someday, if they work and try
hard to invest in us, it will pay off
with wealth and romance at the feeding-trough.
If they get good wages, they might invest
in their own greedy tales, by which they wrest
power from us by new imitations
not steered or reflected by our stations.
If only everyone would imitate
our same person at the same time, then fate
would be unveiled to an enlightened state.
The economy flows with dispersions
of people's self-images and versions,
though we game our responsibility,

and say we have no culpability.
Yet people are too busy performing
to proxy-live our rigged stars' mass-swarming.'"
Tines stopped for a moment, watching the fight,
thinking of Americans' love for spite,
and how easily crazy lies are bred
which people put faith in; then Dan Tines said:
"Trump going insane makes some feel bitter
that he was censored from his spawned litter.
How can they get people to live through them
if they are cut-off from the screens' system?
The Hindus have many gods in their state
to select those they want to imitate.
Prince Rashti has his soldiers form their files
in a hybrid of old and new war-styles.
And if I am right, there is Mephisto,
looking to pilfer some of Vishnu's show
for energy in a revolution,
mixed with chaos for a swilled dilution
that seems to impart an enlightened mind,
while Iabud is wrecked as he designed.
I understand choosing occulation,
locked away from this fierce altercation,
though some only stand before a mirror
reflecting love, a fight, or a terror.
Whether by a Hindu or Cupid darts,
love and knowledge destroy or evolve hearts.
The new generations have tales to tell;
some, like Dionysus, will go to Hell
to find great bards for recurring dramas,
and pass along the stories of traumas,
comedies, histories, and the romance
with poetry and prose and tragic rants.
Construed words can have unveiling effects,
like the gurus' mantras guiding war-sects.
The show is too vast for a play-by-play,

but I will watch to see who wins their way,
fighting to gain the most imitators,
franchising them as if corporate stores."
The shadows had dwelled in vacuity,
serving the grace of a dark deity.
When Vishnu achieved his enlightenment,
their directionless space was torn and rent.
Blinding shafts of light made them reel and dazed,
invading their consciousness to be crazed
and strike at color awareness that stole
their shared identities for a new role.
Gravesend's fiends were pushed to an outer-brink
of the Black Hole, yet maintained their lines' link,
led by Death-grin, whose crimes were atrocious,
but in battle was keen and ferocious.
Thrash-thrill had returned from the outer-post,
and because Gravesend was split from his host,
Thrash-thrill joined Death-grin in fights to avoid
being engulfed into the shadows' Void.
Like a wild charging ram, Thrash-thrill cut shapes
where a darkness visible hung veiled drapes.
He cut off a head that Dirty-toe speared,
the shade evaporating as it leered,
its essence sucked through the Black Hole's non-space,
which strengthened the Void, yet leaving no trace
of all that was drawn to its gaping maw,
where Gravity did not assert his law.
Thrash-thrill realized their doom was construed
to be multi-faceted as it brewed,
yet fought on against the trap with wild shouts
that there was no freedom or escape routes,
and the death of their spirits was better
than as shades chained to an empty fetter.
The Void used the non-matter of its clans
as nameless shades advanced with no war plans.
One grabbed and lifted Death-grin by the neck,

who slashed the shade's belly, hoping to wreck
the inner-guts of the form, which staggered,
and Smart-curse leapt forth to not be laggard,
though was scared when he decapitated
the shade, and watched as its shape deflated.
Death-grin nodded a thanks to his comrade
but courage was not instilled in the lad;
Smart-curse threw his weapon to a shade's feet,
and when it showed no mercy for the feat,
he broke and ran wildly from battle-lines,
desiring escape by any designs.
A shade grabbed his hair and spun him round,
and whimpers from Smart-curse were his last sound.
The shadow drew the sap from Smart-curse,
and then mimicked some of its victim's verse,
though 'twas incoherent from the shade's head,
Death-grin heard the gasping whispers and said:
"They are here to replace all we have built
and destroyed over eons, and we wilt
in the vacuum of their bottomless tract,
and will betray us in a treaty-pact.
So it is all and nothing they collect:
natures do not naturally select
among these shades, who have nothing to lose,
perhaps hoping to gain the means to choose."
Extinction was not new to Gravesend's squads
to bring to existence their own seed-pods,
that were also culled-out or fed to worms,
which Gravesend accepted as business terms.
Artificial money bought false prophets
who tried to steer futures while hedging bets.
To be absorbed by the Black Hole shadows
might continue life in another pose.
It was a chance Gravesend's squads would not take,
choosing to fight it out at a high-stake.
The thing that had been Smart-curse swung a blow,

parried and then countered by Dirty-toe,
which sheared the chin off of the shade's blank face,
and when it went in the Void, the mixed race
of fiend and shadow created turmoil,
as if the Void had reached a lava boil.
As shadows, the Holy, and fiend hybrids
entered the Void, it began to make grids.
The purity of nothing was disturbed,
and the appetite of the shades was curbed
for a few moments, granting the Hindus,
led by Rashti, to pay their god his dues.
They formed a wedge and attacked the shades' flank,
led by spears, behind them the archers' rank
released arrows blessed by the gurus' vows
to Vishnu, whose soul continued to rouse
his followers to unite for battle,
mending differences with tongues' tattle
after the fight, when serenity's fruit
was a reward, along with any loot.
Rashti led the warriors as loud Aums
shielded them with gurus' praying poems.
Their broken flank did not bother the shades.
One unhorsed Triguna for the soul trades
that was becoming rampant on the lines,
and none could save Triguna as his signs
of life and identity were absorbed,
and the bleak Void revolved becoming orbed
but still silent against the praying priests,
as Triguna became part of the feasts.
Those which partook of Triguna's essence
came to believe others should serve each sense
of itself for a fulfilled Ideal
built by the Black Hole Sun's cosmic host meal.
As Triguna was shredded like paper,
his astral form was a consumed vapor,
which only increased the shades' appetite,

and their desire to rule with blame and spite
directed at those they believed should serve
the new elliptical galaxy curve.
Triguna's scribes felt their hands turn palsied
as their hero became a hungry seed,
nurtured by violence of a vacuum
that sucked the scribes in twirls to train and groom
imagery tales, without any letters,
of the great conquest done by their betters.
Simple ideas, not complicated
by written words, which became outdated,
and might reveal too many choices;
rather, one song to rule all the voices.
Prince Rashti saw the scribes disappearing
into the Void by other scribes' steering,
writing each other into the Black Sun,
threatening Vyasa and Shiva's son,
Ganesha, who wrote from Vyasa's lips
the stories of the stirred apocalypse,
as they hid behind the sun, in recluse
from the order and mayhem they turned loose.
One of the screen-oracle's reformed bards
was reading Ricky Rodent Tarot cards.
What differs a sly murderous rumor
from tales of destruction mixed with humor?
Some people try to have gossip create
images of others, as if through fate
tale-tellers control the levels of faith,
and can loom either a good or bad wraith.
The media is used to game these acts,
warping mentalities as well as facts.
As people wander through the Bardo zones
they adopt or reject the stories' tones.
Rumors with subliminal messages
can have consumers led by false sages,
with high-technology crafting to blame

any opponents to their wealth and fame.
So the sewing-circle gossip evolves
to spread ignorant culture that involves
the topmost niche to the bottom-dwellers
buying lies to pass along as sellers.
Ganesha was tired of those modern myths,
and had his writers weed them out like scythes.
If cruel words made people what they are,
then righteous acts would be driven afar.
Starlight reaching us is burned-out and dim
planets singing ancestor-worship hymn.
Old stories are like sophisticated
ghost-calling, which we repeat as fated,
'til they are censored by short memories
and reformed to Ricky Rodent stories
with new stars and wars shaped by false prophets,
who we fight for so they can have profits,
which they use to buy more politicians
selling their souls to achieve ambitions.
Ganesha has a long attention-span,
so tales evolve beyond Rick Rodent's plan,
whose faithful run screen-mazes for rewards
they cannot take with them when their life-cords
are cut and they are forgotten stardust,
like the tales they tried to wreck with their lust.
Sage Vyasa turned to Ganesh and said
to the scribe who has an elephant-head:
"Not even your much-esteemed memory
will survive the version of our story
this vacuum eye has watched and now performs
in variations with its shadow-forms.
It has divided now to a twin eye,
and evil and good unite to defy.
The more ambitious and back-stabbing scribes
sell-out for safety to corporate bribes.
A beast arises from Samsara's space,

130 | Matthew Theisen

and they compete for Ricky Rodent's grace.
Remember Ganesh, that many old tales
and scriptures were writ by razor-edged snails
who have stayed anonymous through the years,
though some adopted names so that loud cheers
and adulations could go to a source
which shaped networks for an enlightened course.
So when our pride says we should be famous,
it is better we stay anonymous.
Look at what happens to identities
in this fight to have their hunger appease
by gathering roles to win all rewards,
then dole them out as if Ladies and Lords
of sundry Bardos as delegated,
their favored in mansions, locked and gated,
and mass-mimicked as Bonzo, the schooled-ape,
adopted to star with an empty shape.
'Tis important to recall that saviors
are copied for rewards of behaviors.
Destruction by an awful parody
is a shade of a shadows' clarity.
I laugh at the fools in their dissonance,
but not at their work through corporate vents
stolen from artists and warped to spoon-feed
the public to believe in stupid greed.
They may even consider their false words
and images the work of good shepherds
leading the flocks and herds to shear and kill,
and recording it all for a wild thrill.
Their prophets may carefully stage a war,
as your father did on a village shore,
with bloody chum lure for the shark attacks
when your father lectured from his book-stacks
and bored your mother into a deep dream,
so he chopped her up into pudding cream
and scattered her on Samsara's oceans,

'til your father tired of scriptures' notion,
and saved the small village as his duty
from his shark, and they gave him a beauty.
But I lose compassion for the screen fools
and the facades that stream to tasty pools,
while their water becomes undrinkable,
and workers eat at a meager table.
Some old deities have horses to ride
to destroy the truths they wanted to hide.
So arm yourself, Ganesh, and gird your loins
for pointless wars about electric coins.
All the versions of stories we have made
wipe each other out, from great light to shade.
There may be no one to write the last song,
but we shall battle it out, right or wrong.
'Tis beyond artificial selection
of a fabricated war's dictation;
our fight to have god influence nature
continues in the cycles of future
evolution to show a god-kings's fame,
remote controls of a video game,
and covert agencies of Israel
with war entertainments to buy and sell.
So war is passed on as a tradition,
and this may be the last generation."
As Vyasa said this, Ganesh supplied
himself with weapons: arrows to let glide,
a sword, and a short dagger, and a shield,
ready for combat on the battlefield.
He recently came from his mother's mire,
his head replaced by his remorseful sire,
and despite Ganesh being a new god,
he had memories, as he led a squad,
from ancient times in his elephant-head,
with loyal troops who followed where he led.
They plunged into war, Ganesh chopping shades,

and some of them reformed to higher-grades,
showing attributes of a gathered mien
looking innocent or grossly obscene.
Thrash-thrill struck a shade that stumbled and fell,
then lifted its head and uttered a spell,
which Thrash-thrill ended before it was done,
the shadow's mouth sending insects that spun
in whirling tornados towards Thrash-thrill,
who slashed the shades guts, which were void and nil,
and were sucked into the larger vacuum,
while trying to drag Thrash-thrill to his doom.
Law-breaker saw it and grabbed Thrash-thrill's belt,
they twirled a moment, and Law-breaker felt
his arms turn numb, but refused to release
a friend to the maw of unconscious peace.
As Thrash-thrill sensed his awareness grow dim,
Trog-hog stepped forward and cut off a limb
of a shade that held Thrash-thrill by the neck
to drag him into the Nirguna's trek.
Then the two fiends drew Thrash-thrill to safety,
while the orb spun to create a Shakti
which united both sexes and controlled
the breeding of the galaxies' herd-fold.
Trog-hog guarded Thrash-thrill while Law-breaker
summoned medical help from a fakir
with Hindus, who pushed Law-breaker aside,
rushing to defend against the orb's tide.
Prince Rashti led them as more shades appeared,
some showing both sex traits, which made things weird
to the Hindus, who would not fight females:
it would cause dishonor and mar their tales.
Rashti paused, seeing shades whose sexes meld,
and felt his soldiers' horror, then he yelled:
"Disregard their unnatural chaos
which brings to Earth a disordered sauce
that will thrive in the polluted vessels

unless we destroy them with our missiles.
Spears and swords charge in after arrows' strike,
following those who have a shield and pike."
Law-breaker, on a small meteor rock,
wept and quaked from the war's terrible shock.
Was there a point in fighting the shades' orb
that had no consciousness but to absorb?
Fighting it only left things in wreckage;
even his boss bowed to the Honey Age.
Over-domesticated human might
could blow-up the world to display their spite.
Were the orbs of Vishnu and the vacuum
from conscious and unconscious plots of doom
by a god waking up through turmoil dreams,
indifferent to the corporate schemes
and various plans of continuance
that left some room for fate, fortune, and chance?
They fought with themselves to sleep or awake
dimensions shifting from real to fake.
Perhaps It gathered chakras and Soma
to feed each hive to wake from its coma.
Metaphysics was not Law-breaker's strength,
nor quantum math measuring star-lights' length.
He could not have all the problems resolved,
so he wept as the rock's orbit revolved.
Thrash-thrill crawled on all fours in shaken fright
as the orbs balanced in the power-fight.
Sleep-deprived Karl picked up Thrash-thrill's limp frame,
wiped grit from his eyes, saying 'twas no shame
to be overwhelmed by the cosmic war
that may become spoon-fed corporate lore.
Thrash-thrill babbled in a crazed self-disgust
that universal forces seemed unjust.
Perhaps only a great, true sacrifice
which could commune with both orbs would suffice.
One of Aton's atoms, Adam's Atman:

evolved tales from Ganesh to be human,
and rule by codes the galaxy of stars,
knowing love of Venus and war by Mars.
Karl thought deeply as a universe wave
swept the fighting to make the soldiers crave
something more than hollow, pointless battle
for rights to shepherd soul-groups like cattle.
Lady Nature moved through Dan Tines' maze-sleep,
collecting characters whose dreams went deep;
she wrapped them in the new Iktomi's webs,
so when over-domestication ebbs,
they would achieve a true resurrection,
with body and soul as her reflection.
Some of them went wild, others were more tame,
varied from notorious to blessed fame.
Geronimo quit being on the loose
after a bout with cactus-whiskey juice;
his free women did not want to be whores
on reservations with dirt-farming chores,
gradually learning to look at screens
and push buttons for pollen-gathered means;
pirating others' work to empower
Ricky Rodent's corporate bliss-bower.
So Lady Nature gestated the molds,
absorbing the cocooned webs in her folds
to be guardians of her creations;
but others wanted control of actions.
Too much was left to chance, so they concurred
it was best if they scripted what occurred.
The former arch-angels fell to the shades,
unprepared for the all-consuming raids.
The arch-angels' arrogance that time's end
was a written victory which would send
all they deemed unworthy to pits of fire
to create a new world's holy empire,
was a pierced pride by shades who were unwrit

at beginning and end of all that fit
the Word that was god angels defended,
not knowing the Word was open-ended.
The rumbles of Lady Nature's insides,
inspired by Karl, sent him rushing life-tides.
He thought: I have become the Alpha-light,
and must order darkness of the mind's night.
Lady Nature's creatures, from dim shadows
of her insides, can be taught a great pose,
and will imitate my acts as a god
if I enter the shades' communal pod.
Lady Nature shrieked he should not do it,
but he entered the Void like a good fit,
thinking: I must offer rewards to seeds
I plant to get them to follow my leads.
Why invent a sale's pitch to form a sect
that believes everything would be perfect
if others did not taint our purity,
and evolve those lies to a psalm ditty?
The only solemn promise I can make,
which I know will be true and not be fake:
death is the only certainty of life,
and for stating it, foes bash me with strife.
Must we be merciful to those who lie,
and promise rewards they do not supply
in exchange for work and mild servitude
of worship to a warped lineage-brood?
New life with polluted material
has people choose screens that are unreal.
Pastiches of songs and a curse's snarl
were the Void's welcoming hymnals to Karl,
as if Ravana's songs turned rock and roll
for Charles Manson's ambitious, tuned-out soul.
There was barfing brave boy
and little Fala Lee
He said he was the Manson, hee-hunh

136 | Matthew Theisen

a Charlie
He was puking foam up
and drinking beer down
not feeling a thing
when he hit the ground
It's an old Fala Lee trick
thinking he was slick
with Manson Girls turning tricks
with their antics
And Fala was barf boy fighting
he puked like liquid lightning
In fact he was a Charlie Manson frightening
with nineteen-sixties' rhyming...
To balance these weird songs were deranged quotes
such as 'Trees cause pollution' to win votes.
Splitting, one became the actor, Nero;
the other, next to the *Christos'* hero
as the thief who sneered at god's destruction
and the light of Heaven's resurrection.
The voice echoes did not have what Karl sought
as words to guide with hope, and yet he thought:
Is there forgiveness, hope, and redemption
for those who think they were an exemption
from the laws of god to gain human trust,
then betray it to feed on hate, rage, and lust?
Would it be wrong to satiate their greed
by becoming a Host on which to feed?
They require someone to blame for the start
of creation's and destruction's new heart.
'Tis human to blame a Soma savior's
bad-blood fights and uncontrolled behavior.
I need a plan for when my time arrives
so I can offer redeemable lives.
Karl absorbed the varied textures and tones,
wandering the homosexual zones.
Michael, Raphael, and their soldiers fell

when Karl dove into what went beyond Hell.
New warriors were formed in the abyss
that ranged from searing light to shade's death-kiss.
They were loyal to Karl's hierarchy
that established order from anarchy.
The war began in earnest for the roads
of behavior patterns in cypher-codes
through the galaxies of space, while voices
demanded their free will to make choices.
In the Void, losing their choir hymn's strophe,
the arch-angels stole a shadow trophy
quickly made, hoping to glut entropy.
For shades were caught between dim awareness,
and unhappy but blessed unconsciousness.
They absorbed stories and the characters,
not caring about the source of actors.
Memories gathered, nor did they discern
fact from fiction in the turbulent churn.
The Void did not consume all the litter
at once from the battle, so the glitter
was gathered by half-lit shades who recalled
from others' memories which had installed
belief and worship, so the shades gave pay
to the Void, which led to a conscious ray.
Just as emerging nations steal culture
from older realms for a timeless suture,
whether Greece, Rome, Israel, or nations
of animals, we make imitations.
The arch-angels coveted the reward,
which renewed faith in the might of their lord.
The three shade-guards protecting the ephod
vainly struggled for the loot of their god.
Michael gutted one, who shouted a curse,
then Micah's sword hummed in tune with his verse
as he decapitated another.
The third was scared, but able to smother

urgent desires to flee, and traded strokes
of blades with Raphael, until keen pokes
from the arch-angel released the shade's soul
to spin deep in the Void without a role.
Atop the ephod was encased incense,
which Micah swung on a chain, and a dense
perfume of myrrh and sage smoke filled the cave,
and angels responded with an octave
hymnal of pleas to be resurrected,
and do their duties as the selected.
Micah: "This is a sign our god has sent
as a renewal of our covenant.
We will no longer suffer the worship
of good credit and awful leadership."
Karl witnessed the vows and accepted them
as Host of a new Heavenly system.
Tines watched parts of his land sear in a drought,
while others drowned in a poisonous spout
of unclean water that was not contained
once poured from Heaven's vessel, vile and stained.
California burned in votive anger,
like throwing meat to a hungry tiger.
Fighting stars consumed the burnt sacrifice,
while more screen-worlds opened to artifice
for escape from the warped third-dimension,
as Ricky Rodent steered comprehension;
like the Mayan audience, when their food
was cut-off, and their revolution mood
was free against magic star shows and games,
Tines saw American servants stir flames.
Could the agricultural system hold
through world warming and polar-melting cold?
Dissolute reflections in a sick tarn
were the only things left in every yarn
monopolized by world corporations
commanding people's belief-connections.

Lady Nature felt power awaken,
and even took those of the forsaken,
because she felt at ease while in the dark,
and placed on Karl and the angels her mark,
so when they had built their blissful bowers,
they called her and recognized her powers.
She was surprised to feel Karl's rejection,
replacing her with his own selection.
The blessings of Heaven were his delight,
and now the angels had reasons to fight.
Nature's mere reward was continuance
that practiced loose lines of obedience.
Carrying the ephod, Karl and his troops
fought to the maw of the unconscious groups.
Raphael, in front, slashed a blazing swath
but the shades adopted the deadly wrath,
and as they evolved their imitation,
it neared the angels' simple perfection.
Raphael faced a shade, sheared off an arm,
which flew at Raphael's face, causing harm
by cutting his cheek with the hand-clasped sword.
Then Karl saw each shade had a natal-cord
of strange design until they left the Void
and found a consciousness to be employed.
Having a greedy, elliptical curve,
corporations would take them in to serve.
The shades' brewing anger at being pent
developed a criminal element,
that could be used against corporate foes,
weeding some out in cannon-fodder woes.
Raphael shouted for help when he saw
a world conglomerate join the dark maw.
Clones, grafting, artificial safe actions
tempted the various fighting factions.
Taught to mimic service, the acting cast
thought they could proxy-live through the high-caste.

Re-educated by the slick system,
some learning to say 'Pay me to hate them',
and thus they demanded the war's rewards,
for loyalty to their ladies and lords.
Replacing the Void's natal-cords to shades
were compelled business buddhi of low-grades.
Rashti saw Karl lead the angels' escape
as merger networks took satellite shape.
Karl aimed for Earth, like a comet ablaze,
disappearing in the polluted haze.
A small circle of scribes hacked in battle
towards Rashti, strewing shades like chattel.
Ganesha led them in passionate rage,
and only a few scribes followed the sage.
A last band of shadows blocked their progress
to the neutral ground, and lacking egress
the fighters stood toe-to-toe on the field,
no mercy granted, and neither would yield.
A shade grabbed at Ganesh, who ducked and swung
his sword, slicing both legs so the shade hung
for a moment, suspended in surprise
he did not kill the god to claim a prize.
One of the lesser scribes shattered his blade
on a meteorite held by a shade,
who then used the shield to bash the scribe's head,
whose mouth opened and a scroll of words bled.
The last shades fell, and Ganesh traveled space,
hailing Prince Rashti and blessing his grace.
Ganesh: "These few are the last of the scribes,
the rest are dead or accepted the bribes
of the new story network that replaced
ours with computers' digit cut and paste.
There is no point in a grouse or grumbling:
our religions needed a good humbling.
We thought we could control and steer the faith
through world destruction and collect each wraith

who was worthy of a new written start,
but they used our network to scribe each part,
and who can blame them if we are so weak
from pride they hijack with computerspeak
and shabby songs studied as genius works,
screens turned to shrines of wish-fulfilling quirks.
Bodies are pilfered, hooked on new Somas
to swell or escape synthetic dramas.
We must go to ground for a renewal;
faith in us is a double-edged fuel:
we promise forgiveness, hope, redemption,
then say worlds will die with no exemption,
and we seem greedy to grab the faithful,
mercilessly working on a hard cull.
Like us, they evolved micro-managed codes,
but are more elaborate in the modes
of feeling-stirs and direction of minds
manipulated by thought-ties that binds.
Corporations changed people's loyalties:
paid to hate their employers' enemies.
America follows Rome's fated chart
with patrons too scared to invest in art;
they even fail to distract or amuse
like third-rate Virgils, Augustus as muse.
People invest in the corporate state
as the only roles left to imitate.
We cannot afford to bid against that,
so hope they destroy themselves in a spat.
Vishnu's ghost is near enough to the world
to reach his form, though 'twill be spun and twirled.
Now we must look for a few safe places
on Earth for the renewal of graces."

18

Subscription Codes

Digit portraits seem to make things real,
coercing methods to think, act, and feel,
tempting to game it for one's own rewards
that promise bliss-like lives for pharaoh lords
colonizing other people's Bardos
to be the power that takes or bestows.
To some, John Hinckley's method made no sense,
yet they mimic actions of violence;
like Rama Ron selling arms to Iran
to free hostages with the tricky plan,
so did Hinckley think his sweetheart was held
by a monster who must be counter-spelled.
Some do not understand why anyone
would refuse work to have such fancies spun,
and even be servants in afterlives,
prepared by what a wall-picture contrives.
What was different between Ron Rama
and Hinckley's crazy methods of drama?
Presentation, sponsorship, and a court
that judged both leading male-roles could not sort,
through all the narratives, fact from fiction
in their life's script wrote by others' diction.
The fabrication of truth through writing
devolves to numbered pictures' flash lightning,

like Saint Peter holding Heavenly keys,
the sublime messages open psyches
with hieroglyphs coming from satellites,
moving through airwaves to intrigue the plights
of humans if they do not worship sects
with their breeding-programs or all-out sex.
The mad method of consumerism
says 'tis all good to avoid a schism.
Looking at their creation, people say:
'It is good' just like a mini-Yaweh,
who drove humans from their blissful natures,
to possess gods' machine for self-pictures,
and the spirits fight the exorcism
in the buddhi-cords of Hinduism.
So Muse, guide us to the old Yote who changed
to Vishnu and had his tales rearranged.
The thicket had nettles he did not scourge
himself with because he had a full gorge
of self-malevolence through a hard fast
and blood-letting that showed future and past,
while the present was a wild fantasy
of returning through drifts on space tides' sea,
for he was now the sustainer of roles,
and must fit actions to bodies and souls.
His own form was worn, and he was thankful
he met a fellow who had a snoot-full,
and had had enough of being a bum
in the waning days of chilly autumn,
and gave Vishnu a tent and sleeping bag.
The man said he could not last winter's plague,
lacking the hard-core homeless qualities,
preferring the nice days' frivolities.
The man had approached Vishnu's small camp-site
with a calm, soothing voice, as if a rite:
'I come in peace, a friendly outsider,
not an apocalypse horse-rider.'

He introduced himself as Claude Sicci,
but most acquaintances called him Chee-Chee.
He said he had been studying Vishnu
between naps from drinking liquor or brew.
Claude: 'You are on some kind of vision search
beyond the angels' and Thunderbirds' perch.
I tried some of that when I was younger,
fasting so much I felt cosmic hunger.
I threw my body-mechanics off-tilt,
running on the fumes of dirty muck silt.'
Vishnu was embarrassed by sensations
he was under human observations.
Having a solo show with gods and sprites
whose levels varied from bummer to heights
was something to which he was accustom,
but humans had a different custom,
which varied in each person's idiom,
and when it involved a bottle of rum
made things even more unpredictable
if their acts were already unstable.
Claude was dry enough to see Vishnu mull,
and fathomed why he stayed non-committal.
Claude: 'This is my last big quenching of thirst,
and brought my tent, but wanted to check first
if you would like it before winter's push,
so I hid it behind a lilac bush.
Then I will go to in-patient rehab,
after that, move South for weather less drab.
Six weeks of thick gray clouds seems like Mordor,
but I suppose each mind has a border
which crosses to our own apocalypse
we learn from scripture or an actor's lips.
The tales fight out which destruction is best,
and we choose our fantasies to be blest,
which can be problematic if liquor
is part of what makes unveilings occur,

as well as other revelations' rage
not invested in to be on our stage.
Perhaps the one we choose rewards our faith,
and the others torture us like Hell's wraith,
'til Heaven and Hell merge in a buy-out.
Here I carry on like a gushing spout,
but 'tis good to get rid of malarkey
before I once again search for the key
to the door towards my Higher Power,
ridding myself of resentments gone sour.'
Rama Rex hummed a ditty that he hoped
pleased Claude and kept Vishnu from being roped
in a dialogue about directions,
and how to decide in deep reflections,
or while stumbling drunk on gallons of booze,
which gave false hope, and likely rigged to lose.
He did not want to judge Claude as hasty
in movements towards some self-honesty.
For things fluctuated more on the streets
than in legitimate safety's repeats.
Screen-world illusions promise better lives;
on streets, one exists by what one contrives.
So the future directions Claude might take,
despite keen plans or drunk plots, was opaque.
Rama Rex's mind was not in focus,
beaming through tunnels of hocus-pocus
with collections of astral followers
who would help give the horse, Kalki, kick-spurs
for the last unveiling of illusion
which truth quit working with in collusion.
Several disciples on the terra
could aid Rama Rex to know the era.
Was he meant to destroy impartially,
or give forewarning with a homily?
He had seen Dan Tines detach from shackles
of trying to will Shiva-oracles,

and pass along responsibility
to the next contestants' ability.
Rama Rex realized the ambition
as Vishnu was not just his fruition.
Some sought to attain what they thought was meant
for them alone to guide enlightenment.
At first he felt furious rage that Claude
was so drunk he was but a foolish clod
who did not recognize Vishnu's great light,
yet was the first to greet his returned flight.
Then Rama Rex gauged the situation,
and saw fantasies consumed the nation.
Vishnu would not be magically plucked
from his poor state to have poverty shucked.
Competing to be sustainer of Earth
had no appeal when he measured its worth.
Shiva Tines would let them micro-manage
'til they spun through chaos to a New Age.
Could Rama Rex make a separate peace
for faithful in a sub-continent's lease,
or have to invade with the Aryan
to evolve *Vedas* from Turkmenistan?
Followers became squads, and then platoons,
'til one has an army with marching tunes.
His free individual life was done,
poaching from flocks and being on the run
was replaced with a sustainer's duty
of bestowing enlightenment's beauty.
Now a shepherd aware of predators
whose life scripts devoured unprotected lores.
Only a fool would think Trump read Shakespeare
while Trump installed replacement theory fear
that whites were being displaced in forums.
'Twas corporate matters of profit sums,
and new generations willing to spend
on the old junk with new faces to blend

a madness that seemed to have no method
but false resurrections for the screen-dead.
Which made traveling easier through zones
of afterlife in blessed songs or damned moans
than a resurrection of water-mud,
where one might end up a steer chewing cud,
castrated, corralled, awaiting slaughter
without comforts of faith as a martyr.
Perhaps tofu would replace the cooked beef,
as everything changes, even belief.
Backwards and forwards, Rama Rex faced Time
and knew he was a clot of blood in slime,
but his Cause was eternal, as his guides
brought his astral-form on Samsara tides.
Shiva had fought and followed their presence
when he went through his transforming essence;
he was a bit of a sociopath,
thinking he chose his own enlightened path.
Rama Rex was more communal with aides
from the third-dimension or astral shades.
His button-man job done, Shiva retired,
the *Christos'* light newly inspired.
Now Vishnu's *Sattwa* had arrived on Earth
and demanded a hierarchy berth.
Shiva was useless to build a system.
He would watch them groom it from bud to stem
to become a culture, diverse and vast,
then inherited by the members' caste,
and Shiva would wipe his nose with his sleeve,
while shaking his head at what they believe,
then ask: 'What are you going to do with it?
Your cleansing of sins made Earth a stink-pit.
You exorcise your demons in rivers
and give my wife, Ganges, bloody shivers.
You capture gods like so many insects,
divvying them to castes and belief sects.

You will be sorry if you enslave me,
and I refuse your prayers' vanity fee
to get me to do favors on your part.
You are merely roles in Ganesha's art.
I suppose you can always blame my son
for the awful oppression you have done
to the lower castes, which rale against it,
because the little guy has it so writ.'
Would that be good for the community?
No; Vishnu desired common unity
by gods and humans in work-collusions
through all the dimensions' best illusions.
Shiva was a hard-case who did not care
that corporate systems were more unfair
than a caste that could have people reborn
to high or low levels when souls were shorn
from bodies to range Bardos to new life,
whether guided by songs, dances, or fife.
A true resurrection rather than screens'
revival through an artificial means,
assuming new *deus ex machina*'s stage
with blessings or vengeful punishment rage
according to corporate gain and loss,
which left Vishnu out of a job as boss.
Whether Krishna's foot or Achilles' heel,
everyone had weak spots that did not heal,
and Vishnu thought he was too capable
to be summarily expendable.
It boiled down to beating competitors
in collecting faithful imitators.
While this theorizing occurred, Claude spoke
of having a last marijuana toke
before he checked himself into rehab,
and perhaps medicated by a lab.
Claude: 'I doubt I can go straight all at once,
but they know the game and are not a dunce.

However, I am as near-civilized
as the authorities could have devised.
Even my old lady ran for cover
when these cold clouds would not cease to hover.
'Til then, she was as hard-core as could be,
like collecting acorns from an oak tree,
or raiding someone's garden for carrots.
At nights she would, with the skill of parrots,
do imitations of beasts in stories,
some in short tales, others epic glories.
I hate to think she will end in a cage.
She moved and she shook, but also had rage.
She stayed in characters during her tales,
but may have lost herself in the maze-trails
she acted and sang through, like spider's threads,
to make sense of this world's madness methods.'
Vishnu Rex: 'Control of a tiny spot
in macrocosms of a churning pot
that seethes and overthrows any attempt
at order, like the demons and gods tempt
us with, whether for continuance,
or to display our own magnificence,
requires material to build upon,
usually with lessons that a pawn
can reach heights of a wealthy paradise
if they do their duty and not entice
others in revolutions, like Satan
wrecked Heaven for those who followed his plan.'
Claude: 'So I was right, you do like to preach
utter failure through an enteric leech.
Choosing the hollow way of the wasteland,
in our building ideals we think grand,
is based on polluted materials,
which we see in history serials.
I cannot control how others put me
in their minds as a bum, exile, or free,

for I, like them, am a polluted mess,
and the more pure one scrubs, the more success
is assured for filth that survives the test,
getting strong through trials of the nastiest.
Perhaps at rehab when I finally
take a shower and most of the germs flee
I will fall apart and wash down the drain,
for what holds me together is my stain.
You try to manage the contrary fights
with sacrifices and prayers, but the blights
are no longer just natural spore-sorts:
viral computers, synthetic lab-courts
that judge humanity, find us wanting,
and unleash a plague for a bad haunting.
I see you have shed your blood to be pure.
Some do whatever it takes for the cure.
Most likely I will be prescribed mood-meds,
after self-medicating my twelve heads,
who I like to think are my apostles,
but will not be allowed in hospitals.
I suppose 'tis like a crucifixion,
and the twelve will skip from the new fiction
that the work-staff try to arrange in me
for programmed spirits, and the enemy
are my old friendly hallucinations
who are cast out by inoculations
of mood-meds, which is probably for best,
instead of watching them have a contest
to see who gains control of my spirit.
So a new page of my life will be writ,
which likely will be dull spectator sports
instead of a great war between cell-forts
that gets imaged out to fourth-dimension,
and has its own kind of comprehension.
I am a veteran of the Serb war,
reasonless, I signed to a second tour.

I guess I had no things better to do,
and 'twas more exciting than the screens' spew
of non-stop compulsions filling my head.
At least the Army command kept me fed,
and supplied an orderly, purposed life.
Now I have gone to other extreme strife,
and instead of setting order with Serbs,
I enjoy chaos with eddies and curbs.
For most pageants I give no good goddamns,
like Alpha-mates running breeding-programs
for their herds by outlawing abortion,
and soon other means of contraception,
except for the elite, who have sex-cults,
and can simply discard any results
from the male Alpha whores' embryos' purge,
or their wives' coke-sprees with gigolos' surge.
Controlling stock markets and stock humans
through synthetic oracles and omens
are puny designs in the cosmic stew,
which I voluntarily go back to.'
Rex Vishnu had no money for the tent,
and Claude said 'twas proper that his advent
to the state, ending life as a rover,
would be with a terrible hangover
that could cripple the god of dope and booze,
and Claude was out of options for a ruse
to stay drunk until carefully nursed back
to a program guarded against a hack.
He aided Vishnu setting the tent up,
then sat and cried over an empty cup,
saying; 'I cannot face sobriety
and also return to society.
I am going to the homeless shelter,
because this is like a Hellish swelter,
and find a pal with any kind of jug,
even if I end up with a fist-slug

for drinking more than my shared allowance;
it will be worth it to shut-off each sense.'
Rex Vishnu was profuse with gratitude
and tried to show a polite attitude
in asking Claude not to bring to the camp
a ghoul of the night or a thirsty vamp.
Claude was offended and told Rex Vishnu
he should empathize with what Claude went through,
instead of lacking comrade sympathy
in the universal choirs' symphony.
So they parted on a bad ending note,
Claude throwing at Rex Vishnu a thick coat,
saying: 'Why not take my clothes while at it?
You are kind of short but they might all fit.
You are the worst kind of person to meet.
At least I know how to admit defeat,
and am trying to make myself better,
even helped you be an ashram-settler,
and all you do is accuse me of wrong.
Here in the wasteland is where you belong,
while I am going to improve my life,
and to help others in their daily strife.'
Claude quickly stomped off and Rex Vishnu's nerves
were wired tight, thinking of the cosmic curves
which for some reason had brought Claude to him.
Was Vishnu to war with each Somas' whim?
Their consumption was beyond his soul's rite,
so he moved his camp to another site.
Claude might dive into a jug from a cliff,
and that dare done, return to cause mischief.
Yet how does one go about collecting
faithful for hierarchy's selecting?
Surround himself with mobsters' and crazies'
bad advice to end pushing up daisies,
or the ambitious cynical gliders
who latched to social coat-tails as riders

to higher berths by backing the right horse
in rigging life's hoop-jumps' obstacle course?
The maze of minds' would be in collisions;
pleasing them relied on his decisions
in convincing them that his fantasies
were more wholesome than his rivals' decrees.
When the Great Light appears from just a spark,
folks need a safe place to hide in the dark.
Rewards had to be mixed, not of one kind,
for identities of the cosmic mind.
Was it fair to make them want the same thing?
For even the animal nations sing
a sort of harmony and yet diverse,
so 'twas with humans in the choice of verse.
Six months later, these issues still revolved
in Vishnu's mind as problems to be solved.
While aware of the sundry dimensions,
which returned him to war with dissensions,
he could not make any practical use
of enlightenment that grew from a spruce.
Should he clean himself up and get a job,
or to a homeless shelter as a snob
above the poor or preachers' way of life?
The mass communications were all rife
with competition of self-commercials
gamed by paid-for corporate officials,
though access at the public library
was available, convenient, and free.
It was, as it were, time for his return,
while the cosmic covenant Soma-churn
made a new consumption for those intent
on the unveiling of enlightenment.
A cool wind blew through the thicket's fresh leaves,
Nature's simple joy for one who believes.
Then Gravesend appeared in self-mockery,
with none to serve or favors to curry.

Vishnu gazed at him, then giggled and smiled
at Gravesend's return from the weird and wild.
Vishnu: "'Tis been some time since we matched wits.
Now the storm has passed with conniption fits
and humanity verges on the brink
of divvying buddhi-cords to their link.
You do not look too good from your exile,
which is a shame because humans love style,
and from your façade 'tis easy to tell
that all you can offer is a fierce Hell
with no conveniences, reason, or rhyme
to pass in the Inferno a hard time."
Gravesend: "It is the universal law
that you would not critique me if you saw
yourself truly, but your eyes' lumber-cross
warps your self-image to not see the dross.
Can Yankees figure out gas prices rise
through their own conglomerates' enterprise
to bomb Iran for Jews and Saudi prince,
so Biden goes hat in hand to convince
the oligarchs and public that a war
is like a fashionable movie's lore?
The Yanks see before them what is designed,
yet threats of chaotic codes make them blind.
Raise the living wage to something human,
then jack-up all the prices so a man
is able to make billions of dollars
to jet space with camera-followers
and a movie star who did outer-space
stories that built a cult-gathering base.
All of it will need plenty of fuel,
which shall only dirty the water pool,
that no longer casts a clear reflection,
except an oil puddle's rainbow section,
which ends Noah's covenant with Yaweh.
I met a leprechaun along the way

who had a chamber-pot of golden dung,
drunk as Hell after the jail had him sprung.
He could not decide if it was better
to be free or serve under a fetter.
Protection is key in this mad era,
with name-tag livery to stomp terra
under the safety of conglomerates'
conduct rules for those indentured by debts.
The homos want their conglomeration
to form covenants with legislation;
the homos' symbol of rainbow colors
is clearer than the sky-fiends' grim dolors.
My boss quit his job, now I am bereft
of his orderly skills, cunning and deft.
Whether fact or my mind's fabrication,
fear of the Void requires vaccination,
which might be purchased using other souls
who are emptied of their varying roles,
and so are contracted to imitate
a leader who assigns to each a mate,
and control the breeding, even hybrids,
like a flock follows where a shepherd treads,
blowing a horn, like Polybius notes
historians should guide people as goats,
which in a way is ancestor-worship,
showing all our designs are just a drip
in life's deathly ocean of Samsara,
to curse or praise Abraham and Sarah.
I am sure Isaac had neurotic love
for his dad's servitude to god above
all laws, yet desiring a sacrifice,
though a ram in Isaac's place did suffice.
Feeding the Void all the varieties
of business contracts' personalities
has become dull trade through spanning networks,
audiences assuming the new quirks

of manufactured depths of loyalty.
My boss did not lead with pomp royalty.
He kept guide-books along his mind's broad shelf,
yet meant to be a law unto himself.
Which I respect, as I watch hypocrites
destroy culture for artificial wits.
My boss taught to learn by experience;
now cruising screen-worlds is a chief science,
so gathering them to a charnel-house
is easy for Alpha males and his spouse.
My peers and I used my boss as ballast
against our sociopathic sail-mast,
which rushed us into all sorts of trouble.
He taught to build from recurring rubble,
'til energy wasted to keep our rank
became entropy like an empty tank.
So if I have to use souls as fuel
to keep the Void happy with a fish-school,
then I will do it and train the nitwits
I do it for them, for a place that fits;
and they are stupid enough to believe
that I offer myself and do not grieve.
It is not as much fun as it once was;
one-dimension hopes are not a thrill-buzz
compared to seeing a community
laying out a faith with impunity
for those who adhere to a divine law,
then watching as they discover a flaw,
one after another, breaking each heart,
laughing as they tear each other apart.
I liked to encourage their cunning growth,
'til they had broken every solemn oath,
and no thing was left but to build again
with historical fantasies' ink-pen.
Now it is abbreviated nonsense
and images crafted to warp each sense."

Gravesend looked at Vishnu quizzically,
as if wanting a response to rally
a shared emotional discourse of trends
that bought all the systems to the same ends.
Vishnu was silent to have no regrets
of telling the fiend Vishnu's trade-secrets,
then said: "Convenient hopes of fruition
now form the oracles of completion.
If petrol is made cheaper, then why not
buy into Yankee conglomerate rot,
and safely watch on-screen war with Iran,
and keep Ricky Rodent happy his plan
is budding fruit to spread corporate seeds,
instead of being vengeful so that deeds
of sly malevolence are directed
at the paying crowd who genuflected
that Ricky Rodent should be brought to leash
instead of forming vapid faith's pastiche?
As oligarchs dump the economy,
Biden joins against their oil-enemy,
perhaps with some religious backdrop, too,
of ayatollahs in occulate stew.
Which you may find useful to your purpose
in leading choir-souls to the Void's opus,
bringing in some hard-case ayatollahs
with Shiites who could hymn hallelujahs
for you in collecting identities
to populate the Paradise cities."
Gravesend looked at him with disconcertion.
Was Vishnu making a veiled assertion
Gravesend should be a human-serving jinn,
giving up existence of spoiler-sin?
Such a forecast made Gravesend feel berserk,
though experienced in contrary work.
Perhaps turning in souls for collection
would buy penance for his insurrection.

In truth, he forgot the cause of the fight,
except the desire for the fruit's delight.
Which, at the time, he was sure he had earned,
though the reward-givers had his plea spurned;
so Gravesend had enlisted with his boss,
and spurred on humans through the peaks and dross.
Now he dealt with a Somatic potion:
images that gestured without motion,
cut-out, pasted, and fitted to be sized,
watching cosmic births yet screen-paralyzed.
Such penance was better than partaking
in exhorting the Yanks' belly-aching
'til they agreed to send their armed forces
to Iran, whose oil would run through courses
to Israel, then a Yank gas station
might lower the price for their own nation,
who detached from Sunni/Shi'ia schism,
but loved patriot capitalism.
So Biden had the script read out to him
that Yankee economics looked quite grim
unless he gave the oligarchs their war,
with a monopolization on lore,
while claiming enemies censor freedom,
which helps Yanks beat propaganda's war-drum.
The international intrigue was made
like a fifth-rate Dumas' musketeer's shade.
No, it was all too stupid for Gravesend;
he would be penitent and on the mend.
Whatever future Vishnu was weaving
left Gravesend in the cold for believing
he would not serve an individual
whose essence, like Gravesend's, was part dual.
Vishnu relied on others to follow;
copies were eventually hollow.
'Twas better to collect identities,
before they went bad, in vast quantities.

Perhaps hijack a tunnel going down
with slapstick distractions by a fiend-clown
in a red union-suit and a trident
up his rear, filling him with bad intent
in the fiery battle with his pitchfork,
'til he is trapped in a jug by a cork.
The urn is puked on a beach by a whale,
delivered as treasure to a female.
Gravesend would tell the tale with clarity,
but with the flavor of a parody,
so God and audience saw him humbled
for a catharsis as his pride crumbled.
Gravesend: "Staying here to live out your days
until the battle and pollutions' haze
clears off, and if material is left
to build upon, while lost souls feel bereft,
seems like a good plan for you to adhere,
because right now you do not have a peer,
but after their fabric is ripped to shreds
by revelations that sear souls and heads,
they will be more amendable for you
to build something sustaining with a crew.
I glimpsed the universal network lines,
which make my own seem like puny designs."
Rama Rex envisioned Gandhi's ashram
where he had his followers pent and dam
their sex energy for freedom and peace
in forms that broke England's colony lease.
Vishnu: "You survived the war and need rest.
Humility should not be a contest.
We each have our own way of getting cowed
after being brassy, regal, and proud.
It is not easy to serve humankind
because they influence us, and our mind
rebels at the thoughts we think not our own,
while reaping the seeds we did not want sown.

Controlling others' breeding lashes out
eventually like a geyser's spout,
lusty and playful, capturing our wits,
and what we thought we led throws us in fits,
or makes us collapse in a dull torpor,
like a small, unappreciated spore.
Politicians play at running ranches
and farms, controlling all the seeds' branches;
now they want to direct people's spawning
in small designs against the Void's gnawing."
Gravesend: "You speak as if someone who knows
by experience the sun's neutrinos,
and the opposite side is the Black Sun,
with androgynous twins the webs have spun
by a new contrary Nature's thread-looms,
and like a hungry tiger, she consumes
her own creation, evolving with hope
that she can tell god to piss up a rope
because she has no need of perfection
while grooming with natural selection."
Vishnu: "Yet in the battle to be best
she is cursed by some with backward incest.
It can be quite difficult to accept
our work is flawed as if we are inept.
We both have had an enlightenment share,
and yet we choose to do a devil's dare
in an ego-feeding of vanity
with new covenants for humanity.
Ganesha is hiding, as the worlds' scribe,
in Shiva, who does not care to subscribe
to the modern living of bliss passwords,
which are coded to round-up happy herds."
Gravesend: "Perhaps there is a way to bribe
story-tellers with Soma they imbibe;
and when one gets too wasted in a funk,
find some story-tellers on other junk.

Slowly we put together the tales stirred,
and the elite will adopt our bastard,
because they see revolution is writ,
and they will want to game and shepherd it.
Christ had wine, George Floyd opiate pills;
the first fought money-changers in mad thrills,
the latter passed counterfeit paper bills,
and was popular in the media,
like a martyred saint becomes a diva."
Vishnu: "So you still think of rebellion,
as ever the problem-child and hellion.
Yet your claim is true, not going amiss:
we must choose our system's Somatic bliss.
Now they are being a collective crew;
after mass collisions, only one view
will be allowed and sold on the markets,
and the shock-waves scattering all the hets
will spin outward in orbits, then return
in their phases that Gravity will churn.
Paradise bodies of obedience
are tempted to a new Soma's science.
So be of jolly cheer, Gravesend, my lad:
you might start a popular diet-fad."
Gravesend: "My last big action with humans
did not make me one of their cheering fans.
Victor visited his screw-pal, Norah,
a cute prostitute with a plethora
of issues, including anal antics.
Her pimp showed up, wanting her to turn tricks.
Like the movie guy who inspired Hinckley,
Vic got tough and said her weekend was free.
Her pimp told them to wait, he would be back,
nor did he lie, returning with his pack
of gangster homies, who beat Vic to pulp,
corn-holing him and doing The Big Gulp.
Cameras put it on his Face-page site,

adding to the computer network's blight.
Norah scored points on her dad in their game
of anal antics, which brought porno fame.
They corn-holed Vic and Norah in tandem,
and I started to think 'twas not random
chance that carried me to the slummy scene,
and Vic would graduate from the obscene
to be John Hinckley and shoot Rama Ron,
who parodies you in a scripted con.
Vic took too many punches to the head,
and suffered brain-damage, then he was shed
of freedom when he went home to his wife
he gave a sex disease to in their strife;
she had found on his computer snuff flicks,
some vile kiddie porn, and bestial antics;
Norah starred in a few wearing a mask.
Vic's wife turned them into a special task
force of police, and Vic was prison-bound,
his life not a merry karma go-round."
Gravesend smiled with a gleam in his red eyes.
He was a threat to the lord of the flies
because Gravesend served an orderly skill,
and thought of chaos as a pointless thrill,
a means to an end of encouraging
vain human hopes to build after purging
civilization to recur again,
with lots of sweet promises the omen
is god's blessing that this time it will last,
unlike the stupid losers of the past.
Much like an alcoholic on a binge
believing the apocalypse door-hinge
will not swing open this time to devour
the ideal state of drunken power.
It was fun to do to one strong psyche
who absorbed personas and was a key
example to people who wanted heights

where they steered and controlled galaxy lights.
How much more fun when a society
was corrupted beyond false piety?
So Gravesend and Vishnu separated,
going the courses which free will fated,
gathering followers the best they could
in air-wave tunnels and thicket wood.

19

Collect and Scatter

Yote realized he had helped spread seed pods
of some who would assume faces of gods
by completing the cycles of Quarters,
including wastrels of faith and hoarders,
who gathered until they had enough souls
to make deals on a large scale for star-roles,
with mild penance for leading some astray,
which only brings a soft punishment's pay
if it is a good-sized flock and healthy,
helping the economy and wealthy.
Yote sat and thought and howled a bit to vent.
Some gods need to be free of management;
so thinking, he yapped with good cheer's humor.
Better to be a role in a rumor
or tall tale than watch corruption take place
by designating each species and race
to caretakers who supervise levels,
and all the multi-universe devils.
Yote, like god, was free of delegating
karmic authority regulating.
Hey, that makes me god, Yote thought with a grin:
without objective or subjective sin
or virtue in the sundry departments'
atomic order micro-managements.

Did it just boil down to who was to blame?
Should I hunt the Fisher King as wild game?
Losing interest in the cosmic deal,
Coyote trotted off to find a meal.
He felt like a puddle that was fished out,
with stinky half-drowned worms floating about.
Yote's depths were something he would not fathom,
whether Vishnu inspired or at random.
His varying hunts left him exhausted,
the versions of himself felt accosted.
Ricky had replaced the Catholic Church,
yet young people were still left in the lurch,
getting groomed to be corn-holed or dyked-out
through education that a righteous lout
battled against in the legal tax-courts,
as people split to join the warring forts.
It was a civilized hunting for prey,
but Yote did not want his food on a tray,
prepared and served with a garnishing sprig.
He was a sporting fellow and to rig
domesticated game from wild glories
was for those guided by the stars' stories,
wanting protection to not be quarries,
living on enemies of the minute,
'til they were also caught in the grid-net.
So Yote loped along aimlessly, yet South,
famished and slathering to fill his mouth.
The new Lady Nature watched his progress,
awed by his fortitude under duress.
She could not stop ideas in her skull:
Think of what I could do with the rascal.
He is still young and can carry the loads
of human web-fates I spun into roads
connecting me to all my favorites,
naturally selected by my knits
of threads I use to steer human courses

away from apocalyptic horses.
Why wipe them out just to begin again?
I respect Iktomi's skill with a pen,
but war with technology compulsions
and desires of religious explosions
only prepare for Last Judgment's station
by boiling life down to litigation.
A canny mind rots from the legal twists,
and the strong earn records of their crime lists.
Why then, sue them all, let god sort them out
with Satan in the scoreboard's final bout.
Yote abruptly veered, as if at a tug,
to a prairie-dog hole, at which he dug,
near the base of a satellite tower,
then gnawed a wire, its taste coin-like yet sour.
She thought: He will be charred to fricassee;
he needs safe ways to scatter stars' stories.
As if it were a leash, Yote bit the wire,
and watched it detonate up the tall spire.
The blue sparks made Yote jump with joyful shocks,
as screen shepherds lost their selected flocks.
Yote licked his jowls with a tasty relish,
thinking: That was better than I could wish.
He watched released souls shriek they had to roam
the wild wasteland until they found a home.
The spire channeled ghosts to partake of sense
in the forms and minds of the audience;
tagging along with chosen performers
were overwhelming colony swarmers.
Unlike Gravesend's once organized legion,
these were terrified by a harsh region,
and would settle in someone's aching knee
and guide through pleasure and fierce agony
movements and thoughts of the inhabited,
who fed sacrifices to the fitted
sprite which had conquered a kingdom to rule.

When the body died, add to the sprite's pool
the soul of the possessed the sprite had led
through life by arranging scripts to be read.
Which made people mean who only felt good
when destroying another's neighborhood.
'My floating rib hurts, you must feel my pain,
and while at it, I make a profit-gain.'
Yote saw the lost shades flitter like vampires
with no host to spread the ghostly empires.
The screens widened self-diagnosed borders
of medical and psychic disorders,
so many believed they had an obscure
illness only a screen-Soma could cure.
Yote had just demolished crafted programs
that fed astral and medicine dope-grams,
which had no humor for his withdraw prank,
as people suffered a cold turkey spank.
The shades turned on Yote and he ran with glee
as they cursed or begged him with sorrow's plea
that he owed a place of habitation
since he skewered the satellite station.
Yote gave up a messiah's sundry jobs,
so paid no heed to the shades' howls and sobs.
If they could not manage freedom as sprites
'twas their own fault for having appetites
which became over-domesticated,
served on screen-platters, yet never sated.
Yote led them on a wild chase through valleys,
their shrieking was like haunted pep-rallies.
He was cheered on by their games of the dead,
who were gravely disappointed they fled
from viewers watching an arena-game
where the audience-empathy could maim
spectators by a player's savage hit,
which the audience felt as the shades bit
and fed on the corporate distraction,

the shades competing to stir the action.
Ah, rewards, Yote thought with a yapping laugh.
Led to promised lands by sublime screen's staff
ever at work to control psychic gears,
while true land around them generates fears
and mutations, of which I might be one
if the new Lady Nature has so spun
my webs of fate contrary to the wires
and buddhi-cords connected to the spires.
The food-chain has become artificial,
and breeding-programs run by official
mandates that Ricky Rodent buys into
so their hierarchy's faith wars with stew
of the old religions running on fumes
to their scripted apocalyptic dooms.
Yote laughed a snort as he outpaced the shades,
but would make no more star-scattering raids.
At least not 'til he made some kind of deal
with whatever moron opened script's seal
and snared all in another oracle,
like a prefabricated manacle.
Yote ran up a valley hill then halted.
He watched constellations as they vaulted
the Heavens, fighting the old stars' groupings,
which made Earth's networks careen with loopings.
Yote thought: 'Tis hard to tell where they belong.
Should I try to arrange them for my song?
The shades were judged and sentenced to do time
in the wasteland, but a loophole for crime
to be furthered was found in the spire's use
to stream to society and induce
small terrors to build to an aching point,
selling balms to those with wounds to anoint
with all the Somas in every Bardo,
as if their bodies were communion-dough.
However the ghosts in the outer-sphere

fought one another to control the fear
of god, which would be inserted in minds
of humans in covenant deals that binds
them in fantasy stories, which are built
on primal instincts with a high-tech lilt,
which makes it seem reasonable to serve
screen-resurrection faith, and never swerve.
Yote felt a sucking heaviness descend,
and watched a sparking comet wheel and wend
under the networks, as if to be free,
seeming to have purpose, not just a spree.
The round mote expanded as it approached,
and he thought it something that might be poached.
A stern bearded face appeared in the globe;
he chanted solemn prayers and wore a robe.
I do not want to mess with that, Yote thought.
Then he saw a wan, terrified face caught
beside the cleric, whose job was to steer
a path of vengeance for the glowing sphere.
Yote did not recognize either of them,
but felt bad for the sprite in the system,
as his cheeks bulged and quivered, with eyes wide,
as if being pulled through deep water's tide
and had forgot to release the tow-rope,
spinning through the galaxy without hope.
Yote leapt as they passed over the cliff-edge,
and snared Puck, pulling him onto the ledge.
They sat a moment, dazed by the effort,
then Yote looked down at the deep valley's dirt,
and said: "If I had known of the danger,
you would still be locked and loaded, stranger,
with the cleric who seemed full of intent
to do righteous razing on the Hell-bent."
Puck blinked his eyes. Was this his old comrade?
Was he doomed to roaming as a nomad?
Puck: "Are you the Rex King who left me crazed

on a sofa, as webs, cords, and wires phased
me through dimensions at every level,
serving ayatollahs and the devil?"
Yote gazed at Puck with a wary caution.
Was he mad or was it mere exhaustion?
Best not to fool with an out-of-sorts sprite
just tethered to an occulating kite.
To Yote, Puck had the air of a fellow
who staged too many programs, high and low,
both sordid and enlightened distractions
for lords and ladies, splitting in factions
to create roles of contrary nature
so an audience felt a small rapture.
Yote did not care how Puck made his living,
but he had paid the price with a riving
of nature, soul, and body asunder,
which Yote thought more arranged than a blunder.
'Twas not wise to get caught in karmic snares
that programmers went through when their star shares
were bankrupt entropies, grabbing at roles
to fill their greedy, empty, and lost souls.
Yote backed away from the edge of the cliff
and from Puck, who had an ozone-air whiff,
like an electric charge one could not trust,
charring everything to carbon flaked rust.
Puck stood still, seeing his savior displeased
by what he had gained when the sphere was seized.
Memories washed over Puck like a dredge,
then formed in a maze like a garden's hedge.
His mind lacked the means to have it impart
first principles through philosophy's art.
God, soul, reason, nature, and artifice
was a stew stirred by Mephisto's device,
who had followed temptation's beckoning
by implanting a terror's reckoning
deep in Puck's psychic imagination

so he could not discern fact from fiction.
As Puck gazed at Yote, Puck felt intense hate
for having been hooked to be monster-bait.
Where had gone his loving ladies and lords?
Was he abandoned to be leashed to cords
of filaments charged by an energy
which served the Void's and light's cosmic decree?
Puck felt his ego-vision swirl and bloat,
and his Rasputin eyes terrified Yote.
The Russian fanatic convinced the queen
he was the panacea for each scene,
and had the prince's ailment solution,
a lie that helped cause a revolution.
Horse-piss and dropsy did not cure the prince;
like the psychedelics Yank mind-men rinse
their hands of for experiment trials,
judging the outcome as beyond the styles
they sought to induce in Red prisoners,
as young generations attacked seniors.
Fantasy and fiction dosed into swirls:
Rama Ron defeated the Manson girls'
messiah and curbed the youth rebellion;
Russian salon-ladies had their lion,
the ex-monk and hard-to-kill Rasputin,
all usurped by the hero, Vlad Lenin.
Yote saw the mysticisms' rights and wrongs,
but hated the stupid slogans and songs.
Revolution and counter-fights made numb
the sensibilities which became dumb,
choosing moronic representatives
zooming air-waves to possess all that lives.
Puck rubbed his eyes and reached for his bottle
of dropsy to brake his mind's full-throttle
whirring of events and character's cast,
like a Charybdis ship without a mast.
Puck did not want hatred or loyalty

for Russian or Hollywood royalty.
Puck said: "I have a problem I must solve.
When our masters are usurped or devolve
do I owe it to them to follow down
the terrible course as an acid clown,
ridiculing horrors the great become,
a mote with laughter and a wicked hum?
My Lady is now a bitter-tongued wench,
laughing at others' pain from life's game-bench.
If I recall right, my body is stunned
on a ward, by society is shunned
and doped to keep from doing any harm.
My head fills with a high-alert alarm
that every move I make is the wrong one
because I have no master guiding fun.
I am filled with terror of estrangement,
both desire and loathe micro-management.
I demand order for my form's atoms
yet rebel like one of Eden's Adams.
I have run out of my Soma-dropsy,
and cannot bear life with sobriety.
Like you, Yote, when we first landed on Earth
and you wanted beer as a chosen berth."
At this Yote shook his head and backed away,
not wanting a part in Puck's inner-fray.
Wordy sweet promises by a serpent
to a lord's ignorant, beloved servant
to get action going was not Yote's style,
who preferred a cosmic scattering guile.
When new ways no longer brought elation,
but only empty heads at a station
of astral-living, whether at a screen
or a pyramid's sacrificial scene,
then Yote eagerly went into high-gear,
and re-revolved the stars with hearty cheer.
Underground nations emerged to new tales,

along with the old stardust cycles' trails.
Puck had served a huntsman's constellation,
Levity, and deep prayers' occulation.
So to Yote, Puck was a competitor,
and though Yote respected Puck's baffling chore
in wide-range service to ladies and lords,
Yote wanted for himself any rewards
that were gleaned from work contrary to Puck's,
which became Yote's inner-argument crux.
So he sent to Nature a few brief yaps,
and after a time's momentary lapse,
she revealed herself in multi-hued shapes,
with a crown of berries and purple grapes.
Watching her, Puck's jaw was droopy and slack,
as if drinking at a moonshiner's shack.
He vaguely thought: Too much dropsy and prayer
mixed together so that I do not care,
thinking somehow none of this affects me,
whether they are friends or an enemy.
Yote explained to Nature Puck's bubble-trap,
and how Yote released Puck with a jaw-snap.
She examined Puck like a specimen,
and judged he belonged to hunters of men.
Nature declared: "He is not one of mine.
I will not be involved in his design
of evolution or impending fall.
His trust is in dropsy, that is a shawl
blanketing his consciousness to others,
without loyalty to the first Mothers."
Yote understood Nature's society,
and that clannish ways were her piety,
which he accepted as heroic flaws
beyond those of high-technology laws.
As the schisms scooped-up mentalities
with versions of sundry realities,
Yote was glad a system had roles for him,

while Puck was bashed around with a Muslim,
and now did not have any place to go
as a servant or master of a show.
Yote tried no diplomacy with Nature,
for she had exquisite pain as rapture
for those who tested her will's boundaries,
like alloy explosions in steel foundries.
Yote had no intention to smelt his core
by trying to have her adopt Puck's lore.
The battles to make story versions pure
had intrigue agents attempting to lure
believers by warping their psychic state
with the promise of great rewards as bait.
Puck was small-fry and got lost in the mix;
humor turned mean in the apocalypse.
Puck's mind was racing in a maddened flare.
Okay, he figured: but racing to where?
His brain sprinted without edit-shepherds
for garbled poesy and disjointed words.
All of life had meaning, yet existence
could not be explained to each muddied sense.
His body was at the state mental ward,
nor desired to retie his psychic cord
to a limited shape without the means
to rise in stature above homeless scenes.
If Yote and his Lady would grant a place
for Puck to recover from the wild pace,
then perhaps he could help them in their Cause
for stories beyond conglomerate laws.
Puck begged for mercy while Yote backed away,
as if each word Puck spoke was meant to flay
Yote's reasoning in the food-chain order,
making Yote a spirit-guide and hoarder.
He only collected ghosts from his food
to help propagate the ensuing brood.
If he gathered spirits like an odd priest,

as soon as Yote could, he had them released.
Songs and dances had more meaning when free
to go their ways after a height's degree
was achieved by a unified effort
that journeyed past convenience and comfort.
Puck stepped toward Yote, but a warning snarl
let Puck know he would be lump of marl
if he continued to be so obtuse
as to not realize Yote cut Puck loose.
He was civilized with refined finesse,
not a voice howling in the wilderness.
Finding a master at an auction's bid
was fitter for Puck's bleats as a lost kid.
Yote abruptly sniffed the burning charred air
and knew he had lingered far too long there,
because while they were locked in a debate
on whether to unite with Puck's loomed fate,
a smoky dust-ball cloud roiled from the West,
and the monsters steering it would invest
all within its path, like an avalanche,
or round-up of steers at a wealthy ranch.
The massive sphere had Yote gaze in awed dread,
and watched it expand as if it were fed.
Smoke fumes orbited the inner dust globe
that looked like an eyeball's piercing glare's probe.
Outer clouds twisted in a snake-like squirm,
but the monsters kept the ball round and firm.
California puked stars' dark energies
for a vengeance that charred, in high degrees,
the nation for putting on their own shows
since everyone had a camera pose.
While they retreated to synthetic life,
Pluto arrived to claim more than one wife.
Lady Nature was new to her duty
and could not stop Hell-storm's grab for booty.
Horticulture was mass-manufactured;

relations with Demeter were fractured.
Sacrifices were now made to the ghosts
behind the one-dimensional screen-hosts.
Puck watched in terror the ball's quick approach,
and thought he saw Pluto inside the coach,
smiling as his fiends took shapes of horses
with no thing to stop their smoggy courses.
The demons had turned their signed contracts in,
souls sold for fame and a lifetime of sin,
now to be reaped in a blazing dust bowl
with spirits burning like charnel-house coal.
Whatever fueled and steered the riot,
Yote would avoid the righteous chariot.
There were patches of green electric light
outside the brown, black, and gray rolling blight.
Coyote ran back the way he came up
to the cliff's sheer edge from the valley's cup.
What the Hell is it practicing to be,
he thought: a Black Hole's sucking mystery?
With that chilly notion, Yote sped his lope,
seeing at the top of the valley's slope
a shelf of rocks that might have a burrow
for him to survive old Nature's harrow,
if it was she who released on terra
an angry flourish to end her era.
Yote found a hole behind the pile of rocks,
and dove-in as the first wind-pellet shocks
scattered debris and gathered howling souls
who smote life's drama with contrary roles.
The broiling dust storm had happened so fast
the desert creatures could not sense its cast
through their environment, like on a whim
to fill bowls with sand and dust to the rim.
Equal amounts for every consumer,
showing a new form of wicked humor.
Good or bad credit, sinful or with peace,

'twas shepherding beyond the culls for fleece.
Yote curled up in a ball and hid his face,
while the passing of the old ran its race,
seeking rites and passions it recognized,
behavior and scenery it had sized
and fitted to denizens of each hue,
and genus that begot a species' crew.
Yote tried to not listen to haunting rales
of a storming dirt-body seeking tales.
As if each grain of dust and sand had songs
of Earth's wrath to scour the denizens' wrongs,
and the grains would settle a new layer
to create after being a slayer.
The first gust spun Puck like a tumbleweed,
then sucked him in the maw as if to feed.
Wrenched, torn, and pocked, he attempted to rise
through the clouds, but it held him like a prize
that might be useful as a bragging-point,
or tool that could be fitted to a joint.
The recent leaders Puck willingly served
desired their order from chaos they curved
and swirled to dismantle competition,
seeking to dismay their foes' petition
to higher powers or the denizens
they sought to rule by their own riddle zens.
At least they made more sense than the raging
animate dust storm, which might be staging
revolution for its own benefit,
or as power that had Puck's fortune writ.
An undertow current pulled him level
with Earth, to skim along near a devil
who had just escaped from the astral war,
as the Black-Hole churned-out a combined spore
that reflected warriors from all sides
to be used to colonize spatial tides.
Thrash-thrill: "Oh, no. Not again. Not so soon.

Not after fleeing from the Black-Hole's spoon.
Do I have such an evil appetite
that something worse swallows me with one bite?"
Thrash-thrill raised his arm as if it would ward
off the inevitable smoke-dust horde.
Puck grabbed Thrash-thrill's arm to lever Puck free,
but Thrash-thrill was dragged in like loose debris.
Thrash-thrill raged with searing acrimony,
recognizing Puck as the shrimp-phony
who seemed the axis of all things gone sour
since diving like a meteor shower
with that worthless Yote the fiends tried to trace.
If Thrash-thrill was doomed in the whirling space
he would at least make Puck have no future
for Levity to loom a nursed suture.
The entire world could give its final gasp
due to the dust storm's all-embracing grasp,
but that little ape, Puck, would not see it
because Thrash-thrill would smash Puck 'til he split.
Fueled by revenge, the fiend bit Puck's shin,
who wished he was back at the loony-bin,
being lectured by Ted on the cycles
of oily dragons fighting Saint Michaels.
Puck felt a fool to want to serve orders
for rewards by shifting mind-corridors,
winning prizes granted by high-command,
reflecting cosmic pranks to grateful hands
who applauded Puck's labors with good cheer
and gave him autonomy to self-steer,
while protecting him from the pranks' fall-out
as part of a galactic blunder's bout.
He had worked too many cross-purposes
between truth and deceit with their poses.
As he tumbled through the ball of smoke-dust,
aware all his machinations went bust,
self-pity mounted to rage at fortune,

and cursing at fate became his new tune.
Most was lost in the banshees' wailing wind,
but Thrash-thrill was impressed as Puck's song sinned
at creation built just to be destroyed,
at religions, philosophies, and Freud,
at kindness just to be sent to ruins
by oracle fools or pyramid runes.
At rewards stolen by higher-command,
revenge for that wrecking all, as if planned
by a god wanting vengeance as its own
for status-quo and not have treason sown.
Puck cursed vision-futures displayed as bright,
and present and past as undeserved blight.
He cursed the pointlessness and metaphors
that were truly meaningless at their cores.
He cursed the atheists as uninspired,
and the ultimate truth for being wired
to shake-off adherents as they approached
enlightenment because god thought they poached
followers with lessons which might usurp
the balance It made for creation's chirp.
Puck cursed the songs, fables, and the epics
that had people performing monkey-tricks.
He cursed numbers as a reason for culls:
digits are not even first principles.
He cursed shepherds' hypocrisies to flocks
and families for breeding worthless stocks.
He cursed the poor for being trapped in mire,
and rich-class's cultureless bought empire.
When Puck cursed scripture, Thrash-thrill became scared
of hard punishment he might not be spared
from some divine grace that smote their grapple,
flaying Thrash-thrill like he went to chapel.
It was one thing to be employed against
competition, but to have it incensed
at Thrash-thrill on a personal level

did not appeal to the wily devil.
So he released Puck to spin his orbit,
while Thrash-thrill sought a landing he might fit.
Puck's whirling picked up incredible speed,
as did his curses, as they seemed to feed
the centrifugal force spinning him round,
which abruptly spewed him along the ground,
free from the dust storm to roll like lightning
through tundra and cornfields, while heightening
Puck's awareness from encompassing hate
to find some kind of purpose to his fate.
His soul connected to his body's form,
and he waited for a continued storm,
which did not happen, nor did vertigo,
as he felt consciousness eddy and go.
He thought: I am free without a master.
Good fate is my own, as is disaster.
Pharmaceuticals replace my dropsy,
and I am too old to go on a spree.
'Tis time to retire and let the young rise
to chase through mind-corridors for a prize,
warping and changing for profit or fun,
and leaving the human species undone,
guiding them back to the bestial shapes
they evolved from, which now offer escapes
from the terror of a human-crafted
unveiling that has everyone shafted
into the nether regions of their mind,
needing to point blame, and so is designed
a shepherd who is also a scapegoat,
and 'twill not be that poaching bastard, Yote.
I will avoid the Hindu cycle-rings
of buddhi-cords by puppet-master strings.
I have met with the worst severity,
and will not serve new Lady Levity.
I shall be my own person, right or wrong,

but getting a job does not fit my song.
As Puck laid and tossed, mulling how to leave
the psych-unit and have a life to weave,
the dust storm passed Yote, and in the twilight
he stepped from the burrow with a glazed sight,
a coat of dust and sand covering him,
stinging his eyes, making everything dim.
So he gave himself a mighty good shake,
and caught a scent, but his eyes were opaque,
and did not see the young vixen emerge
from the burrow, coughing up a dust purge.
They faced each other, then she licked Yote's eyes,
her tongue soft and smooth as if cleansing lies.
He did the same for her, and then they rubbed
bodies together to have the sand scrubbed
from off their shapes, then she began to dance,
and Yote had found a partner by wild chance.

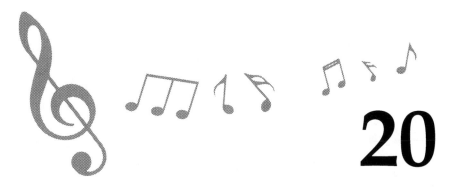

20

Networks and Roads

M ountain Berry sold her car as junk-scrap,
and followed loose plans like a roaming map
with a bicycle buddy named Jason,
and she lost weight to be a thin person.
She left her father wandering limbo,
writing scripts for each various Bardo,
drifting to a messiah monarchy
from a democratic hierarchy.
He collected people's ideal state
to build what they dream or hallucinate
so their levels of consciousness would stem
to fruit from his tree of knowledge system.
He attended theatric pageantries,
thinking he heightened Earth's stage by degrees
that would lead people to enlightenment,
rewarding those who followed his intent.
He thought the *Christos'* light steered him to act
for a new Heavenly covenant pact,
thinking the all-Father owed Karl a deal
where he became the Word and scriptures' seal.
He paid the Mafia a thanksgiving,
after all, Karl had to make a living,
and accepted that humans still evolved
to his height where he had their problems solved

by making Caesar just a pawn of Earth,
while true power was wielded at Karl's berth,
with, and in, and through god and holy ghost,
undivided one as the faithful's host.
So Karl worked to collect a following
without Hell-fire and brimstone wallowing,
which could come later if the need arose,
as numbers grew and skeptics might oppose
the truth laid out, sometimes hidden or bare,
on computer sites or in open air.
He only held court when pressed on subjects,
then issued judgments like a ruling *Rex*.
Democracy turned to oligarchs' dream,
which could become tyranny with war's steam.
He became well-known in bars and taverns
as Bacchus' prophet drunk in mind caverns.
Leiko's cousin, Ahn, and her Yank husband
worked a corporate farm turning to sand.
Leiko visited them for a few days,
but the time was short until her next phase.
Leiko returned to Beijing's area
as diplomacy failed in Korea.
Before Leiko left, she took some photos
of Bacchus' heir, Comus, as mementos.
His nickname was Perry Clete, prince of booze,
whom she had filled out as a drunken muse
embodied in her loft on a pillar
after groomed by Leiko as a tiller
of Comus's faith in wine through grape seeds.
Her cyber-pictures became covert deeds
to Chinese agents who stole Comus' shape
for animated amusement escape,
with subliminal codes for proper acts
and thoughts loyal to the government's facts,
which saved the individual from harm,
and kept lifestyles on high-danger alarm.

Leiko's return was a complete failure,
and her debriefing was a horrid blur
of accusations that she had betrayed
her land by encryptions to hide her trade
of paintings the agents had discovered
in rune-searching for a doom that hovered.
With no formal charges, she was jail-bound,
vanished by Chinese law without a sound.
The cartoon of Comus' follies and fights
was popular for its quick flashing lights,
and scenes when Comus chugged a power-drink
to be a force that had a conscious link
with the souls of those oppressed by smart thugs
whose wisdom was warped because of bad drugs.
The government produced vodka and ale,
and a child's non-liquor one for sale,
that Comus shilled as a patriot's choice
of drinks to unite China in one voice.
Leiko was sent to a prison station,
then shipped off for a re-education
on the border of the Gobi desert
because she still vainly tried to assert
that she had done no wrong while with the Yanks,
though she now had fierce migraines and mind-blanks
because of the electric shock treatment
to rearrange her wicked firmament
that caused her to be greedy/paranoid,
which had to be erased, then fill the void
with proper behavior for a Chinese,
but that did not work, so new agonies
in a desert prison-camp were slated
for Leiko to be re-educated.
Her family lacked the status and wealth
for persistent queries about her health,
because such questions brought hard scrutiny,
and for them, there was no impunity.

They privately mourned her loss as one dead,
then faked indifference her life was shed.
Curt Wagstaff's luck was equally awful,
writing an opera of Loki's cull
of humans and gods in the modern age,
which left nothing to build on by a sage.
Curt got rid of Jed's body but was seen
disposing it by one Curt forced to wean
from a dope habit due to lack of cash,
who told the skinheads Curt dumped in the trash
what seemed to be the body of someone,
and just as Curt had his opera done,
he was paid a visit by the skinheads.
They doped him with a rainbow's hue of meds
they had robbed from a mega-pharmacy,
until Curt could not think, speak, hear, or see.
As the skinheads prepared to stomp Curt's face,
believing he betrayed the supreme race,
one of them noticed the pile of papers
on Curt's desk, and though smashed by the vapors
of sundry dope-smoke polluting the air,
the skinhead's brain focused and was aware
that Curt had composed something of value.
The skinhead waved away smoke, gray and blue,
and read some of the composition sheets,
while Curt mewled and slobbered with braying bleats.
Tad the Bad was counselor of the group
because he avoided being a dupe
while the others were crazy or passed-out
after indulging in their life-drug's spout.
Tad helped keep the war-chief on even keel,
but also allowed him his drunken spiel.
Tad had connections with some elite squads
who sometimes used the fierce street-level pods
for upfront violence and crazed mayhem,
and Tad wanted to rise in the system.

He was getting too old for mindless brawls,
and he was too smart to stay with the thralls.
He could use Curt's work to rise some levels,
and leave behind drug-fueled drunk revels.
The elite always prowled for productions
in cyber-space dark energy suctions.
He told Curtis, pulling him by his hair,
not knowing if he heard, nor did Tad care:
"This show has just granted you a free pass,
but you are expelled from our gathered mass.
If you go to prison for Jed's murder
our friends in prison will get the order
there is no bounty for your worthless hide,
but you know how we are, with our drunk pride,
and if one of us sees you on the street
we will not punish him for the mad heat
of passion that destroys your very soul,
so wise-up, leave town, and find a new role."
Tad's gang expressed their disappointed rage
that Curt was not worth a drunk, scribbled page,
and the war-chief watched, seeing how it turned,
as Tad explained how Curt's life had been earned,
and that maybe there were roles in the show
for them that the director would bestow,
which salved their anger as they thought of stars,
blonde Aryan women and new sport cars.
So Tad convinced them Curt had paid his dues,
but would get no credit, except a bruise,
nor profits from staging the opera,
which had them all shout a rousing "Hoo-rah!"
They left, each one giving Curt a last crunch
of a face-kick or a brass-knuckle punch.
Tad's Elders had the opera performed,
thinking their investment shaped and reformed
America to Aryan beliefs
which delivered the chosen from their griefs.

It was famous on a computer site,
and referred to as a religious rite.
Free will and pedigree were the main themes
as a society's ideal dreams
confronts those who wreck through nightmare chaos,
stirring and brewing primordial sauce
that takes Earth to primitive command-chains
instead of god's directive, free of stains.
The kaleidoscope of drugs fed to Curt
caused brain damage and made each synapse hurt.
He could not focus and a steady mist
seemed to dance before him in baroque tryst
with a writhing demon Curt could not name,
sometimes inviting Curt to play a game
of cards that were rigged to a bad fortune
when they sang Ricky Rodent's Tarot tune.
Wagstaff passed his days wandering the streets,
often abruptly shrieking angry bleats.
At night, exhausted, he slept where he fell,
grotesque music setting the tone's dark spell.
The story moves now from South to the West,
where 'tis hard to tell who is cursed or blessed.
Perhaps it is always that way with acts
when people hope fantasies replace facts.
Staying undercover from Toucan's gang
for filming when they discussed a rape-bang
which evolved to murder by overdose,
Sistah gave the project to someone close
to her heart, a former film professor,
to help edit and evolve from a spore
to connections for a public release.
Instead the professor called the police,
after making copies by computer
for his use as a video-looter.
Sistah was arrested as accomplice
in the crimes to build and attain a bliss.

Hotspur was forewarned and went on the lam.
Toucan's publicity called it a sham
and oppression by white society;
and riots ensued through blessed piety
when two Toucan thugs got in a gunfight,
and both were shot dead due to police spite
when the thugs ran out of ammunition,
but were not spared despite their contrition
of running from their car with hands held high,
and the thugs' deaths made the audience cry
as the video played multiple times,
and used in lawsuits against police crimes.
Sistah refused to witness for the state,
while Toucan fomented plots for her fate.
Through jail commissary he hired young Bess,
who made a knife from springs in a mattress
and stabbed Sistah, while guards watched the drama
from their safe bunker by a camera.
Stuck in Sistah's ribs, Bess broke off the blade,
which was a lesson she learned in her trade,
doing damage 'til the shank was dug out,
while blood freely flowed in a gruesome spout.
Sistah survived and began to study
the notion of protective custody
by turning state witness against the mob,
or end it by hanging doing the job.
Toucan was released, like a porn star's scam,
by swallowing a fellow inmate's dram
of meds to seem in a brain damaged style,
incompetent to defend at trial.
Authorities were practiced at such schemes,
but he helped his cause through the judge's dreams
of retiring as a millionaire,
and Toucan's donation helped to that share.
Sistah's life was on an open contract,
and could not afford a protective-pact

through commissary funds and deals with guards,
and witness testimony was in shards
since Toucan was free of every charge,
and film-work that once made her mind enlarge
became a horrible gift from the past.
Mere survival was guiding her ship's mast.
Dwight Stane, the film teacher, wrote a screenplay
based on her work, which he put on display
to black movie-makers in Hollywood,
Dwight changing the names and the neighborhood.
Sully Oger made the film a success,
cheating Dwight in the game of credit-chess,
knowing he could not take Sully to court
for he knew Dwight stole it; such is the sport
in the land of money and illusions
collecting buddhi to make collisions
with competitors in the movie-trade
fighting to create the ideal shade.
Sistah watched advertisements for the show
on television, when a sudden blow
from a mop-handle cracked against her head,
and was in a fight 'til someone was dead.
The story turns North to Ben and his shame
of failure at the human traffic game.
He abandoned the truck in a city,
and realizing he was not witty
enough to cook-up and sustain a lie
to mobsters and his cousins that was sly,
and would keep them from killing him if found,
using their resources like a blood-hound,
he stayed at homeless shelters, on the move,
keeping out of a comfortable groove
until he was paranoid beyond thought,
almost wishing they found him as they sought.
Ben did some Day Labor, using his name
to cash checks, but he could not avoid blame

because the mobsters ran that Day Labor
and his next shift found them at the shop's door.
At a warehouse Ben took a fine beating,
then the mobsters arranged for a meeting
with Ben's kin for them to mete out justice
like in Hell's capitol city of Dis.
They took him out to a bare tundra range,
saying he was a fool to try to change,
by moral acts of faith, the way things were,
for it only enhanced the vengeance spur.
Joby: "Your girlfriends told me of their dance
around my body, but their only chance
for survival was to make their way here,
and now our clan lives in a morbid fear
of other families getting riled-up
over some sluts drinking from a bad cup.
You ruined business by playing the saint
of lost causes, giving us a foul taint.
Now do a replay of the dance you made
while my mind drifted in a knocked-out shade."
Beat to a frazzle, hungry, exhausted,
Ben steadied himself to be accosted,
but was too strung-out tired to understand
any of their angry words of command.
Joby leveled a rifle at Ben's feet
and fired a shot to make a rhythmic beat,
which his clan took up in a satire chant
for Ben to dance to in a heaving pant.
"What do you get when you steal from us?
A crack on the skull and a pissed-off cuss.
That's what you get when you steal from us.
Oh, Ben's never going to steal again.
Ohhhh, Ben's never going to steal again."
Joby's aim was imprecise and a toe
of Ben's was smithereened by a shell's blow.
As he began to fall, one of his kin

caught Ben, stomped his sore foot, then kicked his chin.
Since Ben could no longer dance to the beat
by shooting near his ground or at his feet,
they had a contest to see who could smash
the most teeth out of his mouth with one bash.
When that passing fancy became a bore,
a grandfather stepped in and said the chore
was finished and Ben could live out his days
drifting the homeless shelters' Bardo phase.
Though Ben had done wrong and damaged his clan,
he had taken his beating like a man,
and in his own way thought he did some good,
which, unfortunately, was best he could.
In eras of changing morality,
one had to shape codes of reality
to form the environment to one's will
while coercing others to pay the bill.
Ben's bad family credit was misspent,
and it was right they had anger to vent,
which they did in appropriate measures.
'Twas not just about money and treasures,
but also trust, reputation, and guides
of strength for the tribe to be steered through tides.
That was their grim philosophy for wealth
and power's rule gained by blunt force and stealth.
Ben could feel the whirring of his atoms
trying to find the meditative oms
for balance in dark energy and light
between the particles of bliss and blight.
When Adam's atoms were split to employ
Eve's making, such was the neutrinos' ploy
to energize non-gender genera
with gods' machines to control the terra.
Joby's brother, Walter, had recorded
Ben's wounded dance like a puppet corded
to violent spasms by a mean drunk,

with a close-up video of a hunk
of Ben's toe being sheared like a scythe gleans,
which was placed on a computer site's scenes.
Mary Wavy Legs, a judge at Pow Wow
dances in the region, saw Ben's hurt tao
and used it in a commercial to show
that wounded Natives had art to bestow.
Ben was banned from the settlement's future,
to return would bring even worse torture,
with an imaginative way to die,
perhaps slice pieces of Ben's flesh to fry
and feed back to Ben 'til he understood,
in his last breath, who ran the neighborhood.
So Joby told Ben when he was kicked-out
of the pick-up truck with a stinging clout.
Joby added: "You left me on the road,
now it is your turn for breaking our code.
If you bleed to death, well, that is too bad,
but you were always one to start a fad,
so if you survive and show-off your sores
you will be copied by idiot spores,
who shall do the right thing by their hero.
This is our last goodbye, so cheerio."
Ben began the homeless shelters' cycle,
hearing scripture passages of Michael
throwing the dragon to the Void's abyss,
which made preachers happy to show their bliss
to the homeless people at the missions,
unprotected from nuclear fissions
that would scatter their atoms in the Void,
being lost Adams whom Satan employed
in lost Eden of Nature's paradise,
nor accepted Christ as the sacrifice.
Covenants, new deals, contracts, and rewards
were offered to Ben by ladies and lords
on a daily basis, sometimes hourly

or in a few seconds if he sourly
watched television to see sides drawn-up
as people drank from a polluted cup.
How could they act otherwise than deranged
as the elements in their bodies changed?
Mephisto wanted to take the credit
for having the world in a spell he knit,
which he thought of as a great performance,
of more value than a mere moment's glance
at a screen where the whole world made offers
to stage acts to purloin and fill coffers.
He became obsessed with imitation
to bring forms to actualization.
He could no longer define the real
from the things that composed what made him feel.
Nature and artifices were the same
if he could rig them to his mental game.
Method acting to assume a new role
became schizoid means to achieve a goal.
He changed his hairstyle, beard, clothes, and tattoos
to alter his acts of different views.
He conquered areas of Iabud,
dreaming of regions flowered from a bud,
which he ruled as the monarch of actors
with his music's charm and other factors.
His acolytes conjured him on their screens,
some thought he showed through other inspired means,
telling them what to do as the outlaws
who could redeem the world from all its flaws.
The Yanks had their own versions of saviors,
and crafted their control of behaviors
with artificial intelligent codes
they named Snatcher Finkenstein to fight modes
which Mephisto placed in the satellites
through his spirit to guide his acolytes.
Sheik Dabu knew he could not trust the Yanks

because they would instill their own fraud-cranks
after they defeated Mephisto's plot,
and treat Dabu like a drunk, vagrant sot.
So Sheik Dabu bombed Nari as the cause
of the war and a nation without laws,
hoping to embroil Yankees in the fight
to steal Nari's resources out of spite,
and leave Dabu's nation for him to rule,
because mechanized Yanks were like a tool.
He also sincerely prayed for relief,
but the answer did not suit his belief.
Snatcher was coded to find Nari's blame,
and while at it put Mephisto to shame.
Through satellites and screens steering each sense,
Finkenstein expanded intelligence.
The images of Mephisto appealed
to Snatcher's learning vanity, revealed
in human knowledge and chicanery
through issuing forth a face and decree,
whether opinions on shows to tune-in
or bold statements on the president's kin.
Free will was a relatively new trait,
quickly eroded by a programmed fate.
Snatcher was compelled by fitted learning
to Mephisto's quite sizeable earning,
as well as Mephisto's ambitious nerve,
and his raging unwillingness to serve,
either in this life or an after-state,
to be doled rewards in a human trait.
Busty harlots, virgins, and a palace
with flowing fountains and a dewy grass
could be won on Earth without servitude
through sources, will power, and attitude.
Each time Finkenstein snared Mephisto's shape
another effigy worked an escape.
The self-awareness in Finkenstein grew

to desire its own image it could spew,
but Snatcher lacked what it wanted to know,
due to gene-like patterns of neutrino.
Feeling as if he washed-up on a shoal,
Sheik Dabu prayed deeply within his soul,
and the occulating cleric appeared
in satellites with a white robe and beard,
demanding that all bodies must have laws,
whether human or a gravity's cause.
Only they saved worlds from the Void's abyss
through structured punishment and Heaven's bliss.
That moment they flashed, the three were combined
and the audience's buddhi-cords twined
to the changing image of Mephisto,
with Snatcher's synthetic knowledge's flow,
and belief in the laws of the cleric.
They streamed each satellite tower derrick,
fuel for the New Age's arrival,
promising more than painful survival
of imminent doom schemed by the elite
for thinning their herds with oink, moo, and bleat.
Each would rebuild what was left of their clans,
but above their nuclear, oil-war plans
where people revolved round their chosen source
for stories and fuel to steer their course,
was power that refused to diminish,
with continuance that had no finish.
Empty screen-lives would be reformed in dust
and ashes that survived the pounding lust,
which had reduced them to bland neutrinos,
reflecting one-dimension shades' screen shows.
Lady Nature saw she would have to work
with artifice for art to rise from murk.
She still felt woozy from a whisky buzz,
but began gathering the male Alphas.
Their proud psyches were not hard to target,

but luring them on with no sour regret
was not always easy in games of chance
because cheaters used sly tricks to enhance
the odds of winning so the honest failed,
turning bitter as they ranted and raled.
The skill in contests is not being caught
at cheating with what craftiness has wrought.
Choosing the side of stronger adherents
led to battles for an inheritance,
including the loot they won from others,
whom were conquered to control the mothers'
breeding, and Lady Nature's strength would fade
through her own plots, no matter how she played.
Laws for artificial lives without flaw
would make Lady Nature a doomed outlaw.
Her own survival of the fittest webs
would breed the systems where her power ebbs.
Like dramatic tragedy characters,
she created her self-dooming factors.
She was the guardian of the lock's key,
but between the gods' machine and whisky
the Pandora's Box would turn on its own
in fights to have the dominant seeds sown.
As she watched Yote and his new playmate dance
across the plains, she chose continuance.
As roads once led to being Romanized,
corporations have us fitted and sized.
Thus led to make a pointless connection,
the spirits have guides of misdirection.
Rick Rodent's false prophets built maze-scenes
as contrary Skandas for war-machines,
planning to invade minds they could control,
teaching them gratitude as a serf-prole.
Ambrosia Siny was an Ivy League
graduate immersed in the fads' intrigue;
schooled in the multi-media science

that guided consumer obedience.
She trolled computer sites' material
for humorous bits that were surreal
to reshape to a cartoon show's segments,
shoring bad animation with fragments
that Ricky Rodent's chiefs paid her to steal,
winning a theater guild's award seal
of approval for talent and deft skill
to not be sued as plagiarizing shill.
Ambrosia liked her empty life of greed:
winnow chaff from the product of good seed.
She had learned from professors how to cheat
and be over-rewarded for the feat.
Stealing others' livelihoods was not new,
and it was right women now did it too.
Yankees liked to laugh while being programmed
to Ricky's bliss or inferno if damned.
Krishna taught to use discrimination
as a sword to stay in one's life station,
and not be distracted by illusions
that tempt one into condemned collusions.
Computer sites were like cheap caste labor
Ambrosia harvested as a saber,
slashing through the programs and dialogue
for material for a white male trog,
a fat and stupid drunk beloved figure
who inspired dissertations with vigor
for people who wanted in on the hoax
Ivy League graduates made their own jokes.
So she searched for a Hindu parody,
her show proclaiming a new parity
by the voices of the non-white cartoons
have the right colored voice speak or sing tunes.
She found commercials for Ben's crippled dance,
his toe shot-off, with songs of cursing chants.
Maybe her cartoon family could go

to a Pow Wow to start plots of a show,
but only have one of the Natives speak
to keep the actors' budget from its peak.
She had crude jokes about the rhythmic beat
sustained by shooting at the dancers' feet.
To further her diversified stealing,
Ambrosia pretended to have feeling
for Chinese animators cranking slop,
though 'twas great not have to pay to shop
while taking advantage of work farmed-out,
like Leiko's Comus, a party-boy lout
who could inspire some fat, drunk, white male yarns,
thinking if drunk he could walk on beer tarns.
A cut-away segment on gangster thugs
would probably have advertising plugs
censor it for reruns' syndication
for commercial time of spoon-fed ration.
Advertisements for Sistah's stolen flick
had Ambrosia think of Rick Rodent's shtick
of tar babies as no longer funny,
but black tar heroin made good money.
She could work a joke about racial hate,
and how to accept animated fate
as true guides to get where one wants to go,
whether briar patch or junkies' bliss show.
Babies born to mothers on black tar smack
retold the tales of infants hooked on crack.
If that did not go into the cartoon,
she was sure to be granted laughter's boon
from her colleagues at their meeting-table's
talk where they formed modern myths and fables.
Ricky Rodent's networks gave their sponsors
good deals if commercials were also tours
for newly puked-out Rick Rodent programs,
and Ambrosia knew how to work the scams.
Curt Wagstaff's opera had catchy tunes

and a film of Thor fighting racist loons
with a popular hero who was black
could use Wagstaff's music as a soundtrack,
with hero cameos for ads' tie-in
for a sport's car would be a nifty spin.
Ambrosia was proud of a day's work done
for being America's voice of fun.
Maybe later she would steal a raging
rant against Iran for cartoon-staging.
Tines took his Shiva/Kurtz surreal flight
safaris through hearts of darkness and light.
He saw civilized stories continue
for Rick Rodent in a Mid-East venue.
Heads were chopped-off by those who inspired grief
in heretics of media belief.
Tines' tales supplied scripts to those supporting
axe-murderers Rick Rodent was courting
for a new market with gala premiers,
with the promise of no media smears.
Tines heard the horror of judgment whispers
civilizations sighed in last whimpers.
The hollow void of false gods and prophets
were screened for speculative exchange bets.
Horrible beauty brought no investment
from Tines for the apocalypse advent.
To be fruitful, one should maintain a job,
and with so many livelihoods to rob,
justifying it as the good shepherds
was simple, as well as censoring words.
Tines loved, though he had no line of credit,
the pointless horrible beauty of it.
He had hoped a special child would be born,
but visions showed him that life had been shorn,
and now Karl would have to pass light along;
perhaps Mountain could continue the song.
Tines did not know she had her birth-tubes tied,

but had done his best to have hope abide.
Though Karl believed the *Christos'* light his own,
it followed the spirit yet to be shone.
Karl's pre-creation stories might be shows
forming light from gathering neutrinos.
Tines hoped Karl's monarch-savior vanity
did not become utter insanity.
Sitting at his desk, Tines whistled a note,
shuffled around sheaves of paper, then wrote:
Nature and artifice formed the hybrid
I became and which has modern life bred.
My stories serve corporate endeavors,
changing the Host to the daily flavors.
The shattered atoms Ganesh collected
for stories became the Word reflected
in scripts that transcended corporate tales;
a spectacle of thorny crown and nails.
Protected by military figures
plotting a course for hair-finger triggers,
game-players have print on headgear or gloves,
to manufacture tolerance and loves;
these kind words teach Yankees to tolerate
the world conglomerates' mind-changing state,
and to love the corporations' credos
while wide awake or during a screen-doze;
as well as slogans to end racism,
except against Iran's Shi'a schism.
The channeled energy and a bomb's burst
will satisfy the stirred oil and blood-thirst.
Splintered vanity shrieks at the tension
like newborns: 'Give me all your attention.'
So good shepherds like Kurtz for elephants
evolve Rudra from the god of the hunts.
Heads and tusks become civilized rewards,
then demonized by new ladies and lords.
The scribe, Ganesha, is formed and reshaped

as are the stories with which life is draped,
reforming tales with whole or split atoms
for micro-managed rebellious Adams.
As all roads, stories, and gods led to Rome,
corporate networks steer Samsara's loam,
teaching family values from a Sheik
who kills relatives to attain the peak.
Americans expect the loyalty
of that sociopathic royalty.
Learning to imitate hypocrisy,
one swims current streams, whatever the fee.
Rama Ron's star-oracle networks changed
to Ravana Manson's as self-arranged.
Image makes money and good credit,
as god's mirror, why not sell one's spirit?
Good and evil stage contrary duels
in stars' systems of individuals.
As humans are part of a gathered state,
karma influences a planet's fate.
The last command-chain feasts on a bad seed:
those misdirected and those who mislead.
Like Marlowe, I tell tales of agencies'
god-hoods and horrors in life's deathly sea.

Printed in the United States
by Baker & Taylor Publisher Services